PRENTICE-HALL
CONTEMPORARY PERSPECTIVES IN MUSIC EDUCATION SERIES
Charles Leonhard, Editor

Bennett Reimer
A PHILOSOPHY OF MUSIC EDUCATION

Robert Sidnell
BUILDING INSTRUCTIONAL PROGRAMS IN MUSIC EDUCATION

Charles Leonhard
THE ROLE OF METHOD IN MUSIC EDUCATION

Edwin Gordon
THE PSYCHOLOGY OF MUSIC TEACHING

Robert House
ADMINISTRATION OF MUSIC EDUCATION

Richard Colwell
THE EVALUATION OF MUSIC TEACHING AND LEARNING

Clifford K. Madsen and Charles H. Madsen, Jr.
EXPERIMENTAL RESEARCH IN MUSIC

Daniel L. Wilmot
IMPROVING INSTRUCTION IN MUSIC EDUCATION

THE PSYCHOLOGY OF MUSIC TEACHING

PRENTICE-HALL INTERNATIONAL, INC., London
PRENTICE-HALL OF AUSTRALIA, PTY. LTD., Sydney
PRENTICE-HALL OF CANADA, LTD., Toronto
PRENTICE-HALL OF INDIA PRIVATE LIMITED, New Delhi
PRENTICE-HALL OF JAPAN, INC., Tokyo

the psychology
of music teaching

EDWIN GORDON
Director of Music Education
State University of New York at Buffalo

PRENTICE-HALL, INC., Englewood Cliffs, New Jersey

DEDICATION

To the author it seems only natural that this book should be dedicated to a unique music teacher and to three very fortunate girls who benefited from his instruction. Robert DeYarman, who is now Supervisor of General Music in the Iowa City, Iowa Public Schools, taught my three daughters music in the University of Iowa Experimental Schools at an earlier time. Jaimeson Beth, Pamela Anne, and Alison Carrie are living validity of the fact that musical understanding and musical enjoyment are complementary and compatible.

foreword

Contemporary Perspectives in Music Education is a new series of professional books for music education. It establishes a pattern for music teacher education based on the areas of knowledge and processes involved in music education rather than on the levels and specializations in music education.

The areas of knowledge include philosophy of music education, psychology of music teaching, and research methods. The processes include program development, instruction, administration, supervision, and evaluation.

The basic premise of the series is that mastery of all these processes and areas of knowledge is essential for the successful music educator regardless of his area of specialization and the level at which he teaches. The series presents in a systematic fashion information and concepts basic to a unified music education profession.

All of the books in the series have been designed and written for use in the undergraduate program of music teacher education. The pattern of the series is both systematic and flexible. It permits music education instructors at the college level to select one or more of the books as texts on the basis of their relevance to a particular course.

Continuing the distinguished tradition of research in the psychology of music established at the University of Iowa by Carl E. Seashore, Professor Edwin Gordon has consolidated his own position as an authority in the field. As a result of combining research with continuing direct work with children, he is uniquely qualified to write this important book in the series. His dual role as researcher and practitioner provides him with a rare opportunity to initiate research, replicate studies, and test research conclusions in the classroom.

In the process of writing *The Psychology of Music Teaching,* Professor Gordon has collected, evaluated, and summarized the results of research on musical aptitude and musical achievement carried on over the past forty years. The book not only contains a synthesis of that research but applies the results insightfully to the learning and teaching of music. In addition, it presents a dynamic view of learning theory as a foundation for music teaching practice.

Music educators are becoming increasingly aware of the necessity for developing teaching practices that are psychologically sound. Representing a veritable storehouse of information about the psychology of musical aptitude and musical achievement, this book should be of great value to music educators in reaching their goals. I am confident that it will make a real contribution to the development of a higher level of professionalism among music educators today and in the future.

Charles Leonhard

preface

This book is written for undergraduate and graduate music students and for practicing music teachers. To serve the needs of such a diverse audience and at the same time promote continuity and ease of understanding, the subject matter is divided into two major parts: musical aptitude and musical achievement.

Although the term "teaching" is included in the title, the emphasis of the book is on the learning process. Clearly, the book is not designed as a methods text. Its primary purpose is to provide basic insights into how students learn music. To this end it is anticipated that the importance of consistency between preferred teaching methods and the learning process will become apparent to the reader. Essentially, the appropriateness of a given teaching method is ultimately dependent upon the logic of the learning principles it incorporates.

In 1931, James Mursell wrote in *The Psychology of Music School Teaching,* "There never was a time when music education more urgently needed the help that scientific psychology can give." It can be safely stated that almost forty years later, music educators' professional needs are not materially any less exigent. Hopefully, this book will achieve its intended purpose in addition to that of providing impetus for designing and conducting relevant experimental investigations.

E. G.

contents

xiii

THE PSYCHOLOGY OF MUSIC TEACHING

PART ONE

musical aptitude

CHAPTER ONE

the source of musical aptitude

Throughout history man has been concerned with his origin and destiny. It is no wonder then that he has also been consistently concerned with the source of his special talents. Musical aptitude certainly has not escaped scrutiny at the hands of music educators and music psychologists. Although one might be curious why for the past fifty years or more researchers have displayed more interest in musical aptitude than in musical achievement, it must be recognized that beliefs regarding both the source and the description of musical aptitude should, and do, affect teaching procedures. It is with this realization in mind that a clarification of the nature of musical aptitude is presented in this and the next chapter. As in general usage, aptitude will refer to potential, and achievement will be used synonymously with accomplishment.

The nature-nurture issue has probably had more direct influence on music education than any other single concept. Briefly, and at the expense of oversimplification, concern was about whether the source of musical aptitude is innate or environmentally based. Supposedly, if it could be shown that musical aptitude is innate, the idea that children with little aptitude should receive a musical education would be suspect.

Conversely, if it could be shown that musical aptitude is environmentally influenced, then it would seem to make sense to teach music to all children. A questionable but tacit assumption of many of those who subscribed to the nature theory was that musical aptitude is a dichotomous trait—that is, one is born either with it or without it. Because of the interest in the nature-nurture issue, some relevant philosophies and research findings will be examined.

Early European psychologists who worked near the turn of the century were instrumental in establishing the notion that musical aptitude is inborn. Men such as Stumpf (20), Pear (13), Revesz (15), and Rupp (16), by analyzing the accomplishments of musical prodigies, complemented each other's findings. Later investigators, and even some contemporary researchers, also inferred the source of aptitude through achievement characteristics but in a more objective manner. Haecker and Ziehen (7), Koch and Mjoen (9), and Feis (3), through questionnaire and interview techniques, found generally that 1) if both parents are talented their children will very likely be talented, 2) if only one parent of the two is talented their children will usually be talented, and 3) if neither parent is talented their children will be less talented than they. It was also suggested that males as a group have more musicality than females. Stanton (12) came to a similar conclusion as a result of working with eighty-five members of six families in which at least one member was a professional musician. Their higher scores on the *Seashore Measures of Musical Talent* when compared to those of individuals from less talented families gave rise to the supposition that innate potential is a more potent factor than environmental influence. In fact, Seashore (18) succinctly stated that "there is indication that the inheritance of musical capacities seems to follow Mendelian principles." In his most recent study, which supports the role of heredity in musical aptitude, Scheinfeld (17) investigated the backgrounds of thirty-six well-known instrumental musicians and thirty-six renowned vocalists. For the former group it was estimated that seventeen mothers, twenty-nine fathers, and about one-third of the siblings were talented. For the latter group, thirty-four mothers, thirteen fathers, and over half the siblings were found to be talented.

The results of some of these studies indirectly suggest that innate qualities might not be the sole basis of musical aptitude. The many exceptions to the rule, such as Toscanini, Rubinstein, and Schnabel, whose parents were found to be, by definition, untalented (17), seem to bear out the environmental theory. Further, the fact that the offspring of some talented parents were found to possess only little talent does not particularly favor either theory. Therefore, it is reasonable to assume that musical aptitude is a product of both innate potential and musical exposure.

From empirical knowledge we know that people are born with diverse degrees of every special aptitude—that is, people are not born with equal potential. However, if an individual, regardless of his high level of potential, was not exposed to music, his potential would probably not become adequately developed; thus it might appear that he possessed little aptitude. Likewise, if an individual was born with limited potential, probably no amount of musical exposure could raise his level of potential. Apparently, then, a good musical environment is necessary for one to be able to *realize* his maximum innate potential, whatever that level may be.

In his study of stability and change in human characteristics, Bloom (1) has presented evidence which indicates that intelligence level (potential) is well defined before a child enters school. He has found a high correlation (relationship) between scores earned on intelligence tests in the elementary grades and scores earned by these same individuals as adults. That the influence of preschool training is of great importance to the development and ultimate level of intelligence is supported by such authorities as Bruner (2), Piaget (14), and Montessori (12). There is evidence to suggest that this is also the case in regard to musical aptitude. Fosha (4), Tarrell (21), and Gordon (6) found that the *Musical Aptitude Profile* scores of both fourth-grade students and older students remain stable even after they have been exposed to musical practice and training. Harrington's data (8), on the other hand, support the notion that on an adapted primary level version of this same battery, scores of second- and third-grade students over a period of time would be comparatively unstable. Because the tests are highly reliable, these divergent results may be attributed to the fact that level of musical aptitude is influenced greatly by early exposure to music but after fourth grade or so, "ultimate" musical aptitude is well defined and impervious to practice and training.

Throughout this chapter musical aptitude has been referred to in relative terms. That is, individuals are described as having more or less aptitude than others but not as having or not having musical aptitude. There is evidence to support the position that musical aptitude, like other human traits, is not dichotomous but that it is normally distributed (5). It is difficult to think of people as being unintelligent or completely intelligent; every person we know is either more or less intelligent than someone else we know. In like manner, everyone has at least some musical aptitude. From an examination of score distributions provided with musical aptitude tests, we further realize that a majority of persons have average musical aptitude, fewer persons have above or below average musical aptitude, and only very few persons have very little or exceptionally high musical aptitude. And, of course, there are gradations within these categories. For a test such as the *Musical Aptitude Profile,* percentile rank norms are similar in variability for groups of students from different subcultures and for those who have different musical backgrounds (5, 6). From the data derived from the national standardization of *MAP,* this same test battery, it was found that the scores of groups of students living in different geographical regions and attending schools of different sizes in urban or rural surroundings were quite similar in distribution (5). While it is true that no musical aptitude test is "perfectly" valid, evidence derived from the better designed batteries indicates that among any group of students we teach, there are as many levels of aptitude as a test author wishes to identify. Only by insisting that those students who score above a certain point on a test have musical aptitude do we unwittingly support the educationally unsound "have or have not" theory.

It is also known that each student has different degrees of *various* dimensions of musical aptitude (5), each of which is related to overall musical aptitude. Research has shown us that there are tonal aptitudes, rhythmic aptitudes, and aesthetic expressive-interpretive aptitudes, and that students differ in these aptitudes both normatively (as compared to others) and idiographically (as compared to themselves) (5).

Because of the limited quantity of research, the source of musical aptitude cannot be completely explained. As music educators, then, we should more realistically be concerned with how best to help students learn music and make the most of whatever musical aptitudes they possess than with how to determine the definite *source* of that aptitude. Until we discover otherwise, let us at least be content with the understanding that musical aptitude comprises various dimensions, that it is a product of innate potential and early environmental influences, and that every student we teach can be expected to have at least some musical aptitude which will remain relatively stable after the middle elementary grades.

In order to establish concepts of how students learn when they learn music, knowledge of what musical aptitude specifically *comprises* is essential. Without an understanding of musical aptitude, sufficient for adequate description and evaluation, it is difficult to teach individual students of different potentials. Students learn most efficiently when instruction is directed appropriately to their individual levels of aptitude, whether they are members of music performance groups or are engaged in general music activities.

In our efforts to distinguish between musical aptitude and musical achievement, we will learn to what degree overall musical aptitude is related to other important human traits such as general intelligence and academic achievement. We will discover that, unfortunately, the relationship between musical aptitude and musical achievement (6) is quite similar to that between musical aptitude and academic achievement (5), and that the relationship between musical aptitude and musical achievement (6) is considerably less than that between intellectual aptitude and academic achievement (11). This suggests that many students are not achieving in accordance with their musical potential. Moreover, we will learn that the overall musical aptitude of 20 percent of students who are members of senior high school music performance groups falls in the lowest third of the population at large, and only 40 percent of this "select" group rank in the upper quarter (5). Hopefully the implications of such fearful findings will not only support the desire to improve teaching procedures but also cause music educators to question whether they are meeting their responsibility to all students.

SUMMARY

Musical aptitude is a product of innate potential and early environmental influences. It is normally distributed among students of all ages. The main dimensions of musical aptitude are rhythmic, tonal, and aesthetic-interpretive. Although musical aptitude fluctuates throughout the primary grades, it becomes impervious to practice and training at about age ten.

STUDY GUIDE

1. In what ways does knowledge of the source and description of musical aptitude affect teaching procedures?
2. What are the distinguishing characteristics of musical potential as compared to those of musical achievement?
3. In regard to musical aptitude, how does the nature theory differ from the nurture theory?
4. Explain why all students have at least some musical aptitude.
5. Why should instruction be adapted to the individual musical needs of students?
6. How can instruction be adapted to the individual musical needs of students?
7. Why should the relationship between musical aptitude and musical achievement be greater than the relationship between musical aptitude and academic achievement?
8. Why should the relationship between musical aptitude and musical achievement be similar to the relationship between intellectual aptitude and academic achievement?
9. Explain why so few students with exceptionally high musical aptitude participate in school music performance organizations.

10. Explain why so many students with exceptionally low musical aptitude participate in school music performance organizations.

BIBLIOGRAPHY

1. Bloom, Benjamin, *Stability and Change in Human Characteristics*. New York: John Wiley & Sons, Inc., 1964.

2. Bruner, Jerome, *The Process of Education*. Cambridge: Harvard University Press, 1960.

3. Feis, Oswald, *Studien über die Genealogie und Psychologie der Musiker*. Wiesbaden: J. F. Bergman, 1910.

4. Fosha, Leon, "A Study of the Validity of the Musical Aptitude Profile." Unpublished Ph.D. dissertation, University of Iowa, 1960.

5. Gordon, Edwin, *Musical Aptitude Profile Manual*. Boston: Houghton Mifflin Company, 1965.

6. Gordon, Edwin, *A Three-Year Longitudinal Predictive Study of the Musical Aptitude Profile*. Vol. V of *Studies in the Psychology of Music*. Iowa City: University of Iowa, 1968.

7. Haecker, V., and T. Ziehen, "Beitrag zur Lehre von der Vererbung und Analyse der ziechnerischen und mathematischen Begabung insbesondere mit Bezug auf die Korrelation zur musikalischen Begabung," *Zeitschrift für Psychologie und Physiologie der Sinnesorgane*, CXX (1930), 1–45.

8. Harrington, Charles, "An Investigation of the Primary Level Musical Aptitude Profile for Use with Second and Third Grade Students." *Journal of Research in Music Education*, XVII (1969), 193–201.

9. Koch, Hans, and Fridjof Mjoen, "Die Erblichkeit der Musikalität," *Zeitschrift für Psychologie und Physiologie der Sinnesorgane*, CXXI (1931), 136–40.

10. Lindquist, E. F., and A. N. Hieronymus, *Iowa Tests of Basic Skills Manual for Administrators, Supervisors, and Counselors*. Boston: Houghton Mifflin Company, 1964.

11. Lorge, Irving, and Robert Thorndike, *Technical Manual, Lorge-Thorndike Intelligence Tests*. Boston: Houghton Mifflin Company, 1962.

12. Montessori, Maria, *The Advanced Montessori Method*. New York: Stokes, 1917.

13. Pear, T. H., "The Classification of Observers as 'Musical' and 'Unmusical,'" *British Journal of Psychology*, IV (1911), 89–94.

14. Piaget, Jean, *The Origins of Intelligence in the Child*. London: Routledge & Kegan Paul Ltd., 1953.

15. Revesz, Geza, *Introduction to the Psychology of Music,* tr. by G. I. C. de Courey. Norman: University of Oklahoma Press, 1953.

16. Rupp, Hans, "Über die Prufung musikalischer fähigkeiten," *Zeitschrift für experimentelle und angewandte Psychologie,* IX (1919), 1–76.

17. Scheinfeld, Amram, *The New Heredity and You*. London: Chatto & Windus Ltd., 1956.

18. Seashore, C. E., *Psychology of Music*. New York: McGraw-Hill Book Company, 1938, p. 345.

19. Stanton, Hazel, "The Inheritance of Specific Musical Capacities," *Psychological Monographs,* XXXI (1922), 157–204.

20. Stumpf, Carl, *Die Anfänge der Musik*. Leipzig: Barth, 1911.

21. Tarrell, Vernon, "An Investigation of the Validity of the Musical Aptitude Profile." *Journal of Research in Music Education,* XIII (1965), 195–206.

22. Wolfe, Dael, *The Discovery of Talent*. Cambridge: Harvard University Press, 1969.

CHAPTER TWO

the description of
musical aptitude

Because only a few students participate in a recital, a member of the audience might lament that there are not more students in the school who have musical aptitude. Such a view, of course, erroneously implies 1) that musical aptitude is a dichotomous trait, 2) that it is demonstrated only by performance, and 3) that musical aptitude and musical achievement are synonymous qualities.

In a general sense, technical ability is considered to be part of musical achievement. However, though one may develop technical ability in singing or in playing the piano, none of these muscular coordination tasks is *necessarily* contingent on musical aptitude. The piano and the singing voice are only media through which one expresses musical aptitude, whether at a high or low level. Possessing good technical facility does not mean having corresponding aptitude. Specifically, musical aptitude is the basis for a performer's sensitivity to musical expression and musical meaning, for the way in which he interprets music through his technical ability. And it is well to remember that not everyone develops technical skill commensurate with his musical aptitude, even if given the opportunity.

What then, specifically, is musical aptitude? We cannot define it any more certainly than psychologists can define intelligence. However, we can study the subjective opinions and objective facts offered by others in an effort to develop our thinking about the matter. In this way we can describe in an educated fashion the basic integral factors of musical aptitude that provide the foundation for musical achievement. With such insight we will better understand what degree of musical achievement may be realistically expected from each of our students. The remainder of this chapter is primarily a critical summary of what authorities consider to be the composition of musical aptitude and its relationship to other characteristics.

SUBJECTIVE OPINIONS

In an effort to identify the components of musical aptitude, some researchers have subjectively distinguished the musical characteristics which accomplished musicians possess. Squires (84, 85, 86), Vernon (96), and Gross and Seashore (8), in retrospective analyses of composers' abilities, generally attribute success to "toil and sweat," intelligence, and using imagery to perceive musical sound. Cowell (8) and Benham (2) in their introspective analysis of processes of creating music also suggest that musical imagery is an important dimension of the musical mind. Similarly, Revesz (70) and Stumpf (90) found musical imagery to be a vital part of the makeup of a musician. They also report other attributes which they found to be indicative of the musically gifted. Revesz, working with the musical prodigy Nyiregyhazi, claimed that the abilities to recognize chords and intervals and to transpose, improvise, and compose music are basic. Stumpf found that the young genius Areola demonstrated excellent timbre discrimination, was quite facile in recognizing and using dissonant chords and in improvising nontonal melodies, and had "absolute" pitch.

Because musical achievement can evidently be so easily confused with musical aptitude when musicians' characteristics are analyzed subjectively, it seems imperative that another method of describing musical aptitude be considered. In view of the ethical and practical demands put upon practicing music educators, we must identify an objective way of evaluating the musical aptitude of all students and not just of those interested students who first must avail themselves of abundant training. Musical aptitude tests not only offer a promising method for evaluating students' musical aptitudes but, more pertinently, provide a description of musical aptitude. With this in mind, we will examine the content and the empirical validity of the more popular tests.

EMPIRICAL DEFINITIONS

To be sure, there is no unanimity among those who develop tests either in this country or the world, regarding the design and content of a musical aptitude battery. Music psychologists, such as Farnsworth (17), Mursell (64), Lundin (57), and particularly Lowery (56), suggest that Europeans base their tests on "Gestalt" theory, while Americans hold an "atomistic" philosophy. What this implies is that the British, for example, adhere to the idea that musical aptitude is a unitary, or musically all-inclusive, trait (which they say has a great deal in common with general intelligence), and therefore the component parts (if indeed they agree that there are parts at all) of musical aptitude should be evaluated in totality. Americans, on the other hand, would go to great extremes to try to identify mutually exclusive aspects of musical aptitude (all of which, by definition, must be related to overall musical aptitude) in order to provide independent evaluations of each even though their tests make provisions for an estimate of overall musical aptitude. Although this general dichotomy is ascribed to musical aptitude measures, it will soon become evident that test authors are, nevertheless, eclectic.

Seashore

In 1919 the first standardized test of musical aptitude was published. This battery, the *Seashore Measures of Musical Talent* (80), represents the work of a great pioneer who gave objectivity to some subjective ideas about musical aptitude espoused by his European predecessors. Five subtests were included in the battery: *Sense of Pitch, Sense of Time, Sense of Consonance, Intensity Discrimination,* and *Tonal Memory.* A sixth subtest, *Sense of Rhythm,* was added in 1925; similar revised versions of the battery appeared in 1939 and 1956. The test stimuli consisted of laboratory instruments (such as tuning forks and a beat-frequency oscillator) but not musical instruments. It was evidently reasoned by the author that in order to measure musical aptitude effectively, a test should not be contaminated by factors indigenous to a particular culture (79). Consistent with this psychological construct is the item content of the subtests. For example, the pitch discrimination subtest deals only with pairs of "isolated" pure tones that are intervals of half steps or less, and consequently the items are intended to be devoid of any type of tonality. Similarly, neither of the two series of short pure tones which serve as items in the memory subtest (the subject has to identify the one tone which is changed in the second series) is musically oriented. These concepts also loom large in the time and intensity subtests but not in the consonance subtest. In the time subtest the subject is asked only to discriminate between length of pairs of pure tones; for the intensity subtest the perception of comparative loudness of two pure tones is emphasized.

Preferential responses, rather than objective responses, are called for in the consonance subtest. For this subtest subjects are asked to decide which of a pair of pure tone dyads has more "smoothness, purity, blending, and fusion" (79). Perfect octaves and fifths rather than major and minor seconds and sevenths, for example, are keyed as correct answers, the logic of "correctness" being based on the nature of the overtone series (79). The rhythm subtest also may inadvertently allow a subject to make use of formal achievement in responding to test items. Two series of clicks are presented and the subject is to tell whether these patterns are the same or different. Because, as Seashore suggests, human beings subjectively organize a series of objectively produced sounds (79) (such as the ticking of a clock or the sound of moving train wheels), the rhythm subtest may not be "culture free." That is, musically trained subjects may aurally organize all patterns into duple meter for comparative purposes. Heinlein has shown that a similar type of subjective organization might occur in the *Tonal Memory* test (41).

During the twenty-year period until the Seashore battery was revised in 1939 and for some time after, reactions to the battery were probably generated not so much by the psychological constructs of the subtests as by Seashore's adherence to the doctrine of inherited musical capacities. That Seashore was consistent in this regard is suggested by the deletion of the *Sense of Consonance* subtest from the 1939 version and the addition of the nonpreference subtest, *Timbre*. For the new subtest, the examinee is required to determine only if the tone quality of a pair of tones is the same or different. Cultural bias is less prevalent, of course, because this subtest evaluates only one's ability to hear the effect of differential intensities of particular partials in the overtones series on timbre.

Experimental researchers, culminating with Wyatt (104), were particularly bent on disproving Seashore's theory of "innateness" by demonstrating that scores on his tests are affected by musical practice and training. The literature is replete with studies of this type as most recently summarized by Horner (45) and Shuter (83). From a more practical point of view, however, Mursell (64) and others have offered the following constructive criticisms regarding the battery: 1) Musicians are rarely concerned with discriminating between two pitches nine cents apart (a cent is 1/100 of a semitone). In the tuning of an instrument and, more important, in ensemble performance, good intonation is probably much less dependent on "absolute pitch" than on relative pitch. Ostensibly, possession of the latter ability better enables one to adapt pitches to the musical demands of key and mode. 2) Proficiency in identifying an unfamiliar pitch in a series of musically unrelated pitches does not necessarily mean that corresponding proficiency will also be demonstrated when dealing with a musically oriented series of tones. Supposedly, we hear music as intelligible relationships among sounds and not as a mass of unrelated pitches. 3) Because a musician deals with tempo, meter, and melodic rhythm in a polyrhythmic sense, it is questionable whether the ability to discriminate between the comparative duration of two tones which lack rhythmic qualities would have much relevance to musical aptitude. 4) Similarly, it is doubtful whether a musician would need to concern himself with the relative loudness of two pure tones. In music, phrasing is comprised of the interaction of dynamics, tempo, and tone quality expression.

Followers of the Gestalt theory of musical aptitude test construction further suggest that the battery lacks validity because each subtest deals with only one dimension of music. As assiduously outlined by Vernon (93, 94), they reiterate that most music we hear is made up of the interaction of rhythmic, tonal, and expressive qualities. Probably because of the low statistical correlation among the subtests, Seashore maintained his belief in factorially pure capacities. In fact, he renamed the 1939 version the *Seasore Measure of Musical Talent*s. However, it should be pointed out that a high correlation between any two measures is limited by the low reliability of just one of the measures and to an even greater extent by the low reliability of both.

One can only speculate that Seashore's final thoughts on the measurement of musical aptitude gave impetus to others to develop new aptitude tests during the following decade. Although Seashore held the theory that auditory acuity is mandatory for a musician (just as an artist must possess visual acuity), he did state that success in music is also dependent on other factors that his battery did not directly measure (79). He probably was referring not only to personality traits, motor abilities, and quality of musical training but also to aptitude for fusing elemental capacities into a meaningful musical whole.

More empirical validity investigations have been conducted on the Seashore test than on any other battery; the bulk are of the criterion-related validity type. The question one asks in this type of assessment is how students' scores on an aptitude test are related to their standing on another factor (usually achievement) at approximately the same time. A basic limitation of this approach is that a correlation coefficient describes only relationship and not causation of the relationship. When a substantial concurrent relationship is found between musical aptitude and musical achievement scores, there is no way to determine whether high aptitude (measured after training) is responsible for the high achievement scores or whether the training which produced high achievement actually provided for the high scores on the aptitude tests. Therefore, we cannot establish, solely on the basis of criterion-related validity information, whether a given test is essentially an aptitude test or, indeed, an achievement test. Furthermore, even if causation could be established, information of this type does not necessarily indicate what a test is *valid for* in actual use. These problems notwithstanding, the results of the many criterion-related validity studies initiated by independent researchers (and by choice, not by Seashore who ". . . steadfastly maintained that their internal validity was well established and that attempts to validate them against fallible external measures, such as judgments of omnibus musical behavior, were inappropriate") (78) are contradictory. Some investigators report moderately high concurrent relationships, some report low, and others have even found negative relationships (that is, those who score high in the Seashore test tend to score low on the musical achievement criteria, and vice versa) (57). These varied findings in part result from the use of different types of measures of achievement as validity criteria and are dependent on the reliability of such measures and the insights and research skills of the experimenters.

In the one predictive study of the Seashore test (88) Stanton's reporting was not complete enough to allow for specific conclusions. Because of the manner in which success in music was predicted as a conglomerate (by the aptitude battery, an intelligence test, an audition, past achievement, and the like), it is impossible to determine from the report to what extent the Seashore battery singularly predicted success in music. It is interesting to note that Stanton chose graduation from the Eastman School of Music as a validity criterion of success in music. If it was indeed found that the Seashore battery did correlate highly with the criterion, it could be argued that this would not necessarily validate the battery as a musical aptitude test. Graduation from a music school is contingent upon other factors besides musical aptitude.

Kwalwasser

Midway between the publication of the first and second editions of the Seashore battery, Kwalwasser and Dykema developed the *K-D Music Tests* (49). There is great similarity between the two batteries. Possibly because the ultimate level of attainment of *musically trained students* is best predicted by past achievement, Kwalwasser included achievement measures in the test battery. Six of the ten subtests which constitute the K-D battery were developed to measure the same factors found in the Seashore battery, but they were designed and titled differently. In contrast to Seashore, Kwalwasser employed actual orchestral instruments and the Duo-

Art Reproducing Piano as stimuli for some of the subtests. And although he employed pairs of tones only for discriminatory purposes in some subtests, he did develop musical relationships among tones in the memory subtest. As a result of these and other minor differences, such as greater extremes between tones in the pitch discrimination subtest, the K-D battery has acquired the reputation of being "easier" than the Seashore battery (16). However, if we consider the true meaning of "aptitude," this is questionable; tests either measure the aptitude of individuals in a speci-fied group with *precision* or they cease to be valid for their purpose. This is not to say that special tests cannot be developed to discriminate more precisely among students within a restricted aptitude level.

The six subtests comparable to those of the Seashore battery are: *Tonal Memory, Pitch Discrimination, Intensity Discrimination, Time Discrimination, Rhythm Discrimination,* and *Quality Discrimination* (quality meaning timbre). *Melodic Taste* and *Tonal Movement* are pref-erence measures. For the former, the subject is to indicate which of two endings provides the best tonal termination of a short melody. The latter measures the ability to judge the tendency of the final tone in a succes-sion of tones to proceed to a point of rest. The two achievement subtests are *Rhythm Imagery* and *Pitch Imagery.* For both of these subtests the subject is to tell whether what he hears is what he sees in notational form on his answer sheet.

From an analysis of the Kwalwasser tests it can be seen that the psychological constructs of the battery include musical preference and achievement as dimensions of musical aptitude. It should be recognized however, that for the *Tonal Movement subtest,* the keyed answers are limited largely to recognition of whether the final pitch corresponds to traditional standards of Occidental tonality. The same may be said for an item as a whole in the *Melodic Taste* subtest. And although in prac-tice rhythm typically interacts with melody, the latter subtest is not spe-cifically designed to allow rhythm to influence the preferential response.

Even if musical achievement subtests are found to be highly pre-dictive of the degree of a musician's further accomplishment, they still will have little relevance to our attempt to describe musical aptitude. It is not axiomatic that a test which has predictive validity is necessarily an aptitude test. For example, strength of hand might prove to be an excel-lent predictor of success in playing the string bass, but, strictly speaking, this physical ability cannot be construed to be a basic musical aptitude.

In 1953 Kwalwasser authored another test, the *Kwalwasser Music Talent Test* (51). Unlike the earlier test, only four discrimination factors are measured—rhythm, loudness, time, and pitch—and electronic equip-ment is used exclusively as the source of stimuli. Although four factors are included for the evaluation of talent, the test provides only a total score (not separate subtest scores).

The extent of the stability (reliability) and the interrelationship (intercorrelation) of subtest scores bears on, and ultimately affects, the validity of a test battery. Neither reliability nor intercorrelation data are reported in Kwalwasser's test manuals. Therefore, although Kwalwasser in his original test offers scores for ten different factors, we cannot be sure to what extent these different factors actually exist, nor can we be sure of the degree to which they comprise some unitary trait. Furthermore, in neither test manual does the author offer evidence of experimental validity even for total scores.

Wing

Herbert Wing was the first to develop major innovations in musical aptitude testing after Seashore. An Englishman, he was undoubtedly influenced in establishing psychological constructs for his test by other English authorities such as Burt (5), Vernon (97), Mainwaring (59), Lowery (54, 55, 56), and Semeonoff (82). The *Wing Standardized Tests of Musical Intelligence* (100) include seven subtests. The first three are nonpreference tests—*Chord Analysis, Pitch Change,* and *Memory*—and are concerned with tonal concepts. The remaining four subtests, *Rhythmic Accent, Harmony, Intensity,* and *Phrasing,* are preferential in nature.

The test, which is said to reflect the "omnibus" theory (56), differs from the Seashore battery in two important respects: 1) for each subtest the piano is used as the stimulus, and 2) the item content of each of the subtests is more musical in nature. In the chord subtest the subject is to tell how many tones he hears in one chord; for the pitch subtest he must determine if the second of a pair of chords is different from the first and if it is, whether the difference results from moving one note up or down. For the memory subtest a series of tonally related pitches is heard. Each series has a distinctive rhythm, although this is not relevant to the correct answer. When the series is repeated, the subject is directed to count and indicate which pitch, if any, is altered. In all four preference subtests, familiar melodies are performed as they were originally composed or in "mutilated" fashion. The type of change in the melody corresponds to the nature of the specific subtest. The subject is to recognize whether the performances are the same or different; if they are different, he must choose the rendition he considers better.

The preference subtests might be more properly titled recognition tests because students who have previously heard the familiar music that constitutes the test items might try to determine which rendition of the pair was actually written by the composer or which is more consistent with traditional interpretation.

It appears that the main contributions of the Wing battery in assessing musical aptitude are the use of composed music, the consistent use of a musical instrument to provide stimuli, and the design of the non-preference *Memory* subtest. The fact that the examinee hears the inter-action of melody and rhythm in an item, as he would in music he typically listens to, would allow for a more valid judgment of his tonal memory. Curiously, though, Wing does not include a nonpreference sub-test of rhythm memory in his battery.

The psychological constructs of the Wing battery can help us in our attempt to develop a description of musical aptitude. The three non-preference subtests suggest new ways of thinking about tonal aptitude. The four preference subtests support the Gestalt idea that musical apti-tude is more than just a matter of "mechanical acoustic" perception and that "judicious musical" understandings are to be reckoned with (21). Certainly he has brought the domain of musical sensitivity, in regard to expression, to the fore. However, we cannot be more specific about the nature of Wing's concept of tonal aptitude or of musical preference be-cause reliability, validity, and intercorrelation data are not reported for the seven measures. Only one reliability coefficient is discussed in the test manual, that for the composite score. Wing reports extremely high cri-terion-related validity for the highly reliable composite score (he found, for example, that those who score high on his total test tend to persist as members of musical performance groups [101]), but, like his predecessors, he does not report empirical validity for his subtests. Wing offers norms (in just five categories—A, B, C, D, and E—and not in percentile ranks) for only two scores in his battery: a total score for the three nonprefer-ence subtests and a composite score for the complete test.

As indicated before, a lack of extensive subtest reliability and inter-correlation data and information pertaining to the diagnostic properties of a battery (the degree to which individual subtests of a battery correlate with specific musical behaviors) leaves us in doubt about the extent to which that battery actually includes more than one dimension of musical aptitude. It could be that Wing subtests, though based on strikingly dif-ferent psychological constructs, actually measure one or more highly similar traits. We will take notice of this later as we discuss the intercor-relations among subtests constituting different batteries.

Drake

Drake published four tests of musical aptitude in 1932 (13). The tests dealt with melodic memory; interval discrimination; pitch memory; and "feeling" for key center, phrasing, and rhythmic balance. For this reason we might conclude that Drake, at that time, believed that both auditory acuity and musical expressiveness were important components of musical aptitude. However, in 1954, when the *Drake Musical Aptitude*

Tests (10) were published, only the idea of the melodic memory test (presently titled *Musical Memory*) was carried over from the older battery. The other of the two subtests which constitute the new battery is called *Rhythm*.

The memory subtest utilizes a piano as the stimulus and all items are musically oriented. Drake indirectly emphasized this by calling the subtest *Musical Memory* rather than tonal memory. For this subtest the subject hears a short musical phrase once and then hears from one to seven renditions of the phrase. The "repetition" may be exactly the same, it may be in another key, it may have some "notes" (pitches) changed, or it may have a "time" (rhythm) change. The subject is to indicate the nature of the repetition. To be familiar with the concept of modulation and to know the difference between "time" and "note," which are requisite for adequately understanding the directions for taking the tests, the subject should have had some formal music instruction. Because of this and because both tonal and rhythm *responses* are required in the same test, it is possible that a test of this type could overemphasize musical achievement.

The underlying psychological constructs of the *Rhythm* subtest seem to have little in common with the psychological constructs of the memory subtest. The first part of the *Rhythm* test involves "clicks." The subject hears four clicks of a metronome counted and then silence; he is to keep counting quietly to himself (at the given tempo) until told to stop. The number at which he stops counting is his answer. The second part of the test is exactly like the first except that the subject hears interference in the form of a different tempo beat where he heard silence in the previous test. Undoubtedly, the ability to maintain a consistent tempo (except when altered for expressive reasons) is important to musical undertakings. But, in musical practice, tempo interacts with meter ,and melodic rhythm.

Only tests of high reliability are capable of exhibiting substantial intercorrelations with each other. Both Drake subtests are highly reliable, which makes the low intercorrelation between them noteworthy. Further, when we consider the design and content of each subtest, we should expect them to measure relatively different traits. However, it would be more instructive if we had some empirical evidence that each subtest score is related to different musical behaviors. Drake does not offer information on the diagnostic validity of the two subtests but rather reports criterion-related validity coefficients for each of the subtests based only on the *same* criterion of ". . . expression in playing and the rapidity of learning . . ." (11).

Two distinctive characteristics of Drake's test should be emphasized: 1) Drake provides two forms of each subtest, each differing in difficulty, and 2) norms are offered for both "nonmusic" and "music" students. Music students, as defined by Drake, have had "five or more years of musical training" (11). Theoretically, music students, as a result of their training, should not score higher than nonmusic students on a musical aptitude test. However, music students generally do score higher than nonmusic students, probably because a greater percentage of gifted students elect to study music.

Tilson

Shortly after the appearance of the first Seashore revision, the *Tilson-Gretsch Musical Aptitude Test* was published in 1941 (92). Tilson included only four tests in his battery: *Pitch, Intensity, Time,* and *Memory.* The psychological constructs of these tests are highly similar to corresponding tests in the Seashore battery. Tilson, unlike Seashore, provides criterion-related validity data and norms only for a total score on all tests combined. Both men used heterogeneous groups for deriving reliability estimates for their respective tests. Seashore combined the test results of fourth- and fifth-grade students, sixth through eighth-grade students, and those of high school freshmen through college seniors. Tilson combined test scores of students in nine different grades, four through twelve. (In this connection, it is interesting to note that Drake provides chronological age norms based on two- and three-year intervals from ages seven through twenty-two.)

It is known that, generally, the more heterogeneous a group is, the higher the test reliability will be for that group. But the fact remains that no matter how high a reliability coefficient is, it is of limited value if it is not relevant to the group for which the test is intended to be used. For example, if a test were administered to fifth-grade students to evaluate their musical aptitudes (or for experimental research purposes), we would need to know the stability of the scores of those fifth-grade students as an intact group. Factors other than musical aptitude may affect test results, especially with a heterogeneous group. About all we can tell from a multigrade reliability coefficient is that the single-grade coefficient would generally not be any higher and probably would be lower.

Gaston

A few years after the Tilson test became available, Gaston published the first edition of *Test of Musicality* (26). Its subtests are similar to some found in the Wing, Drake, Kwalwasser, and some unpublished batteries. The test is composed of four parts which yield a composite score, but Gaston offers neither part scores nor corresponding reliabilities. The piano is the stimulus for the complete test. As in the Wing *Pitch*

Change test, in part one the subject hears a tone and then a chord, and he is to indicate if the tone is in the chord. For part two, which resembles the Kwalwasser achievement subtest, the subject decides whether what he hears on record is what he sees in notational form. If the two are different, he must indicate whether a "note" (pitch) or the rhythm is different. Part three is quite similar in design to the Kwalwasser *Tonal Movement* test, and part four is like the Drake *Musical Memory* test but without the "key change" option response. Gaston offers criterion-related validity of the total score on his test for students in various combined school grades. It is not surprising that, as for some academic achievement batteries, separate norms are provided for boys and girls. Considering the content of the test, we recognize that the *Test of Musicality* provides some support for previously postulated descriptions of musical aptitude.

Bentley

By and large, musical aptitude tests have been designed for use beginning with students in grade four (approximately nine years old). Although Drake provides norms for seven-year-olds and Wing for eight-year-olds, Bentley has more recently developed a test specifically for use with children as young as seven years old (approximately second-grade level). The *Measures of Musical Ability* (3) comprises four parts: pitch discrimination, rhythm memory, tonal memory, and chord analysis. The last two parts are designed like the Wing subtests of the same name, and the pitch discrimination part corresponds to the Wing *Pitch Change* subtest except that in the Bentley measure, single tones are used rather than chords. The rhythm memory part is designed like the tonal memory part except, of course, it deals with rhythm patterns. As in the Seashore test, an oscillator is the stimulus for the pitch discrimination section, but an organ is used for the other three parts (including rhythm, even though the item patterns are nonmelodic). Bentley cites statistically nonsignificant relationships among the four sections of his test even though he does not report reliability coefficients (nor validity coefficients) separately for the various test parts (3). (The lower the reliability of subtests, the less likelihood there will be of finding significant interrelationships.) Further, like Tilson who reports criterion-related validity findings based on students older than those for whom his test is intended, Bentley reports total score criterion-related validity based on the performance of older students (some at college level) and professionals, even though his test was specifically designed and developed for use with very young children. As for the Wing test, total score norms are based only on a five-category scale and not on percentile ranks.

Considering the evidence presented thus far, it appears that musical aptitude batteries specifically designed for younger subjects and those for older differ mainly in the directions given for taking the tests (36). This fact is relevant to our understanding of musical aptitude, for it tends to corroborate the belief that musical aptitude becomes, at a relatively early age, noncumulative.

Musical Aptitude Profile

The comparatively new *Musical Aptitude Profile* (33) has been described as an eclectic test (in regard to the "atomistic" and "omnibus" theories) because, while both preference and nonpreference subtests constitute the battery and the test items consist of especially composed music performed by professional musicians, the battery does, nevertheless, provide for the evaluation of seven separate postulated factors of musical aptitude. The musical dimensions measured by the battery are classified into three main divisions: *Tonal Imagery, Rhythm Imagery,* and *Musical Sensitivity.* Two subtests are provided for each of the nonpreference total tests, *Tonal Imagery* and *Rhythm Imagery—Melody* and *Harmony* for the former and *Tempo* and *Meter* for the latter. The preference total test, *Musical Sensitivity,* comprises three subtests: *Phrasing, Balance,* and *Style.*

In the *Melody* and *Harmony* subtests, the subject is asked to compare a "musical answer" to a short but complete musical statement. The violin is the stimulus for the former subtest, and both the violin and the cello are used for the latter. The "musical answer" contains more tones than the original phrase, and the subject is to determine if the answer is "like" the original (if it is, it is a tonal variation) or "different" from the original (not a tonal variation). If the subject is in doubt, he is directed to fill the "in doubt" response ("?") on his answer sheet. The upper part of the restatement of items in the *Harmony* test is always exactly the same; the embellishment takes place only in the lower part.

Both *Tonal Imagery* subtests incorporate a variety of keys, major and minor modes, and nontonal phrases. Duple and triple meter, mixed meter, unusual meter, and a variety of tempos, syncopation, and anacruses are also used. Although particular attention is given to a musically expressive performance and the item content incorporates rhythm as an integral part, on these subtests subjects are called upon to make a judgment only about tonal aspects.

For the *Tempo* test the tempo of the ending of the restatement is played faster than, slower than, or exactly the same (rerecorded) as the ending of the original statement (the melody, of course, is the same in both statements). If the ending of the restatement is played either faster or slower than the statement, the subject simply indicates "different"; if the endings are the same, he marks "same"; and if he is in doubt about the correct answer, he uses the "?" response. For the *Meter* subtest, the subject indicates "same" if the statement and restatement are exactly alike, or "different" if the restatement of the melody is in a different meter than the statement, or he may use the "in doubt" response. Usual, unusual, and mixed meters and anacruses, syncopation, and various tempos are employed in both subtests. The expressive and tonal elements of the items in the rhythm subtests are equally as comprehensive as those found in the tonal subtests. In keeping with the design of the battery, subjects are asked on these subtests to make only a rhythmic judgment. The violin is the medium of performance on the rhythm subtests.

The *Musical Sensitivity* subtests require the student to decide which of two renditions of an item ". . . makes the better 'musical sense' " (34). In the *Phrasing* subtest, each *original* selection is performed a second time with different musical expression, and the subject is asked to decide which rendition he likes better. For the *Balance* subtest the endings of the pair are different, and the subject is asked to decide which ending is better for the selection. In the *Style* subtest the selection is performed the second time in a different tempo, and the subject decides which tempo best complements the tune. Violin and cello are used as performing media for the preference measures. In all three subtests the student reacts to dynamics, tempo, tone quality, intonation, and melodic and rhythmic contour and style, but he indicates only his specific preferential judgment by simply marking "1", "2" or, if he is in doubt, the "?" response.

The psychological constructs underlying the various *MAP* subtests are quite different from those already encountered for other tests. For example, the *Tonal Imagery* subtests go beyond measuring aural discrimination of isolated pairs of pitches or ability to determine specifically which one pitch of a tonal series is different. They are instead primarily concerned with melodic contour as it interacts with tonality and rhythmic elements. The *Rhythm Imagery* subtests also embody unique psychological constructs. That is, rather than dealing with nonmelodic rhythm patterns or isolated metronomic clicks, the *Tempo* subtest allows for tempo to be influenced by, and interact with, melodic rhythm as well as with expressive elements typically found in music. Likewise, *Meter* has similar characteristics, except that in this subtest, meter must be perceived as it influences melodic rhythm. In this sense tempo and meter perception are presented as basic functions of rhythm aptitude. It is interesting to note that the battery, unlike the Seashore measures, does not contain any type of "time" discrimination test or rhythm "memory" test.

The *Musical Sensitivity* preference subtests reflect some ideas of earlier test developers. For example, the *Phrasing* subtest is like the Wing test of the same name, but it consists of specially composed music which elicits judgmental rather than recognition responses. Furthermore, the stimuli are more flexible; this better allows for intonation and dynamics to interact with tempo and tone quality. The *Balance* subtest is like the Kwalwasser *Melodic Taste* test but is designed to allow both rhythm and melody to complement musical form. There is no prototype for the *Style* subtest, which evaluates perception of appropriate tempo as it interacts with musical form and phrasing.

National norms and reliability coefficients are provided for scores on each of the seven *MAP* subtests, the three total tests, and the complete test, *separately* for grades 4 through 12. The fact that there is a low correlation among subtests comprising different total tests and a somewhat higher correlation among subtests of the same total test indicates that the battery is measuring aptitudes which do not greatly overlap. (Two possible exceptions are the *Meter* and *Balance* subtests [34].) That these seven aptitudes are related to specific corresponding musical behaviors has been suggested by independent investigators (22, 40) as well as by the test author (34). A unique aspect of *MAP* is its demonstrated predictive validity. In a three-year longitudinal study (31), the pretraining *MAP* composite score predicted success in elementary instrumental music with unusually high precision. Furthermore, after three years of typical musical practice and training, it was found that students' *MAP* scores did not significantly improve upon readministration.

Relationships Among Tests

Before attempting to reach a consensus regarding the composition of musical aptitude, a discussion of the functional interrelationships among subtests constituting the same and different batteries is appropriate. To aid in this endeavor, a summary description table of the musical aptitude tests already discussed is presented on pages 26 and 27. The entries refer to the function of subtests and not necessarily to actual subtest titles. Subtest stimuli are given in parentheses.

In their critical analyses of the Seashore and K-D batteries, Farnsworth (16) and later Whitley (98) found little evidence to suggest that subtests of the two batteries which bear the same or similar titles (except possibly the tonal memory measures) have much in common. (As for individual batteries, it should be emphasized however that strength of intercorrelations among subtests of different batteries is also affected by the reliability of the subtests.) Drake reports that his *Rhythm* subtest and the Seashore *Sense of Rhythm* subtest ". . . are not measuring the same ability" (11), and in this case, at least one of the subtests demonstrates relatively high reliability. Gordon (28), in a study of the intercorrelation of the *MAP* and Seashore batteries found that the composite scores of the two batteries (both of which demonstrate relatively high reliability) correlate much lower with each other than *MAP* correlates with an objective criterion of musical achievement. Both also correlate only slightly higher with each other than does either with academic achievement.

Within the past few years, some factor analytic studies of test batteries have been conducted. Drake (12), utilizing subtests from various batteries, concluded that tonal memory, pitch discrimination, rhythm intensity, and tonal movement, along with general intelligence, can be considered as a general factor constituting musical aptitude. Wing (99), like Burt (5) before him and Vernon (97) after him, found evidence not only of a general factor (which involves intelligence) but also of two group factors, the first comprising tonal elements ("analytic") and the other musical preference ("synthetic") as depicted by his battery. McLeish's analysis of the Wing and Seashore batteries uncovered a general factor in which tonal elements play an important role (58). Both Faulds (18) and Franklin (21), the former working principally with the Seashore test and nonmusical acoustical tests and the latter with these and Wing's test, supported the hypothesis that musical aptitude has two main elements, "mechanical acoustic and judicious musical." Manzer and Marowitz (60), employing only the K-D test, found two group factors. The two imagery subtests combined into a "musical training factor" and the remaining eight subtests formed a "sensory factor." Dealing primarily with thirty-two audio-acoustical tests, Karlin (47) identified as many as eight group factors; the three most important being pitch discrimination, memory for isolated elements, and memory for series of notes. Like Karlin, Bower (4) found no general factor but rather three group factors. Her factors, which greatly overlapped but were different from Karlin's, included 1) tonal memory, pitch and rhythm discrimination, and melodic preference, 2) loudness and time, and 3) only tonal memory and rhythm discrimination.

ANALYSIS OF THE COMPOSITION OF MUSICAL APTITUDE

There appear to be three main components of musical aptitude. We may identify them as tonal, rhythmic, and aesthetic expressive-interpretive. Empirical evidence indicates that the tonal dimension consists largely of tonal imagery; we hear, recall, understand, and anticipate musical sound through tonal imagery. Evidently, memory of specific patterns, discrimination of higher and lower pitches, recognition of tones

Summary Description of the Nature of Musical Aptitude Test Batteries

	Audio-Acoustical Perception	Tonal Concepts	Rhythm Concepts	Expressive-Interpretive Concepts	Achievement Skills	Number of Scores for Which Norms Are Provided
Seashore 1919–1960	Pitch Discrimination (Oscillator) Intensity Discrimination (Oscillator) Time Discrimination (Oscillator) Timbre Discrimination (Oscillator)	Tonal Memory (Organ)	Rhythm Memory (Oscillator)	Consonance Preference* (Tuning Forks)		6
Kwalwasser-Dykema 1930	Pitch Discrimination (Oscillator) Intensity Discrimination (Piano) Time Discrimination (Piano) Timbre Discrimination (Band Instruments)	Tonal Memory (Piano)	Rhythm Memory (Piano)	Tonal Movement (Piano) Melodic Taste (Piano)	Tonal Notation (Piano) Rhythm Notation (Piano)	11
Wing 1939–1961		Tonal Memory (Piano) Pitch Memory (Piano) Chord Memory (Piano)		Rhythmic Preference (Piano) Harmonic Preference (Piano) Intensity Preference (Piano) Phrasing Preference (Piano)		2

* 1919 version only.

Tilson 1941	Pitch Discrimination (Reeds) Intensity Discrimination (Audiometer) Time Discrimination (Metronome & Audiometer)	Tonal Memory (Organ)				1
Gaston 1942–1957		Musical Memory+ (Piano) Chord Memory (Piano)		Tonal Movement (Piano)	Tonal & Rhythm Notation (Piano)	1
Kwalwasser 1953	Intensity Discrimination (Oscillator) Time Discrimination (Oscillator)	Tonal Memory (Oscillator)	Rhythm Memory (Oscillator)			1
Drake 1954–1957	Tempo Discrimination (Metronome)	Musical Memory* (Piano)				2
Musical Aptitude Profile 1965		Melodic Imagery (Violin) Harmonic Imagery (Violin & Cello)	Tempo Imagery (Violin) Meter Imagery (Violin)	Phrasing Preference (Violin & Cello) Tonal & Rhythm Balance Preference (Violin) Style Preference (Violin)		11
Bentley 1966	Pitch Discrimination (Oscillator)	Tonal Memory (Organ) Chord Memory (Organ)	Rhythm Memory (Organ)			1

* Also includes a "time" change in some items.

27

moving up or down or by step or skip, identification of which one of a series of pitches is changed, or recognition of a change in a specific tone in a chord involves *"hearing"* but not necessarily *"musical understanding"* or *"musical anticipation."* The fact that one displays good pitch discrimination does not necessarily mean that he will have corresponding aptitude in tonal imagery. However, if one does have good tonal imagery aptitude, a natural concomitant would be a good *sense* of pitch. The identification of specific pitch change is a mechanical-acoustical feat, but awareness of melodic contour, which gives rise to tonality and therefore implies musical meaning, involves tonal imagery aptitude. We probably perceive tonal meaning in the form of tension and relaxation as a result of a sense of tonality which interacts with rhythmic elements (in an aesthetic rather than technical sense). It could be concluded that the difference between imagery and memory (or synonymously between aptitude and achievement) is that the former is characterized by the extent to which one intuitively *derives* musical understanding from organized sound and not necessarily by how well one *gives to* organized sound some theoretical explanation.

Similarly, the evidence suggests that rhythm aptitude is best characterized as imagery for rhythm (through kinesthetic response) as it interacts with the tonal and expressive elements of music. Specifically, it seems that the senses of tempo and meter are the primary elements of rhythm aptitude in that they give rise to tension and relaxation in melodic rhythm. It may even be that rhythm aptitude is the basis of musical aptitude. Certainly without sufficient rhythm aptitude, insight into different musical styles remains limited. In the same way that a sense of tonality is basic to tonal imagery, a sense of meter is probably basic to rhythm imagery.

Good discrimination of time and rhythm is not necessarily indicative of corresponding rhythm imagery aptitude, but good rhythm imagery aptitude would involve a good sense of rhythm. Because rhythm memory and tonal memory are mainly achievement factors, the extent to which these memory learnings can be developed may be largely dependent on the aptitudes of rhythm imagery and tonal imagery, respectively. If this is true, time discrimination probably has less relevance for rhythm aptitude than pitch discrimination is believed to have for tonal aptitude.

The aesthetic expressive-interpretive dimension of musical aptitude has received relatively little attention from test developers as compared to the tonal and, to a lesser extent, the rhythmic dimensions. A possible explanation of this may be that generally it has not been possible to deal with this aptitude without unduly contaminating it with achievement. Evidence suggests that the aesthetic expressive-interpretive dimension is the unifying element of musical aptitude. That is, it amalgamates the tonal and rhythmic aptitudes and gives rise to the comprehensive aptitude of musical sensitivity. In this sense, a person might possess high tonal and rhythmic aptitude, but unless he also commands corresponding aesthetic expressive-interpretive aptitude, his overall ability to respond to a *musical situation* will be limited. Musical aptitude involves more than a response to the meaning of musical sound; it also involves response to the manner in which meaning is expressed *musically*. That is, the way something is said is at least as important as what is said. Musical expression minimally involves suitability of tempo, periodic adaptation of tempo and dynamics to the demands of tonal elements, and suitability of tone quality and intonation to the style of the music.

Finally, there is reason to believe that the aesthetic expressive-interpretive dimension of aptitude is important to creative and improvisational achievement. This is particularly evidenced by the inclusion of melodic taste, tonal movement, harmonic preference, and melodic and rhythmic balance subtests in test batteries. However, this does not necessarily preclude the doubt that most, if not all, of these measures *might* be somewhat reflective of culturally conditioned musical achievement.

MUSICAL APTITUDE AND OTHER FACTORS

An understanding of the relationship of musical aptitude to psychological and physical characteristics and to environmental background can further contribute to our understanding of the description of musical aptitude. While it would seem that objective evidence should make such relationships obvious, it should be kept in mind that the degree of relationship is dependent on the validity of the tests and the nonmusical criteria examined.

Environmental Background

As an added precaution in the standardization of the *Musical Aptitude Profile* (34), a representative sample of students in the United States was selected in accordance with the same sampling procedures employed in *Project Talent* (20). In this way, the random sample of students who participated in the standardization program was stratified according to 1) school geographical location, 2) school size, 3) whether a school was in a rural or urban setting, and 4) the socio-economic status of a school district. Analysis of the test results showed no systematic differences in score distributions in relation to these four factors. That is to say, the proportion of students at all aptitude levels was found to be similar for groups of students regardless of significant nonmusical characteristics associated with their school.

In connection with the environmental factor that might be expected to affect musical aptitude most, the results of two highly specialized studies of socio-economic status are now available. In the first, *MAP* results of junior high school culturally disadvantaged students were compared to those of culturally heterogeneous students (27). Students in the former group were technically classified as "educationally deprived" under the provision of the Elementary and Secondary School Act, Title 1. The differences in *MAP* mean scores found between this group and the corresponding group that participated in the standardization program were negligible, nor did the test standard deviations, which give evidence of the variability of test scores, differ in any meaningful way. The second study, especially designed to investigate the predictive validity of *MAP* (31), provided evidence that the correlation between the composite *MAP* score and the occupation of the head of the household is positive but low, and is significantly lower than that between musical achievement and this same *MAP* score. Furthermore, the corresponding coefficients representing relationships of aptitude and achievement scores to college attendance of parents were, as expected, almost identical to those for occupation. Another factor, parents' interest in the musical achievement of their children, can be inferred by the presence of a piano and a record player in the home and the degree to which children are allowed to hear music (either "live" or recorded) at home. All these variables, including the extent to which parents supervise home music practice, are correlated with musical aptitude scores less than are parents' occupational or educational status (31). Further, these same environmental factors generally correlate significantly higher with musical achievement measures than with *MAP* scores (31). From the evidence presented, it appears that although level of musical aptitude is affected by early childhood environmental influences, this aptitude is not conditioned in a socio-economic sense. Students with great musical potential can be found as readily in culturally deprived areas as in more privileged neighborhoods and, conversely, students with limited musical potential are as numerous in affluent environs as in ghettos.

The relationship of aptitude scores to amount and type of musical training was investigated in conjunction with the standardization of the *MAP* battery (34). It was found that 1) participants in school music performance organizations score higher on *MAP* than do nonparticipants and 2) although members of choral organizations score higher on *MAP* than nonparticipants, they display only slightly less aptitude than instrumental music students. However, nonparticipation in a school music performance organization is not a limiting factor in attaining high-level aptitude scores, nor does participation in a school music performance organization assure the attainment of high aptitude scores. These facts are specifically described in the Sandusky prestandardization study of

MAP (34) but they become even clearer through a comparison of the standard score-percentile norms for music students and nonmusic students which are provided in the *MAP* test manual (34). In this connection, it is interesting to note in the *MAP* manual (34) that aptitude score distributions of students who perform on keyboard, percussion, brass, woodwind, or stringed instruments are highly similar.

Data from the Sandusky study (34) indicates that approximately forty percent of students who have had little or no formal music instruction score at the eightieth percentile and above on *MAP*. A similar percentage of students who have had extensive musical training score at the twentieth percentile and below. Evidently, whether we consider the general socio-economic factor or the more restricted musical status factor as an indicator of environmental background, we must conclude that musical aptitude knows no boundaries in that it is not contingent·on favorable social circumstances. We, as music educators, must be challenged by the realization that no matter what group of students we are associated with, we can identify individuals with high-level musical aptitudes which must be developed. And we can expect to find in any group a proportionate number of students with lower aptitude levels whom we must aid by adapting our instruction to compensate for their specific musical deficiencies.

Psychological Characteristics

As suggested by Cox (9) and Stanton (87), performing musicians, music educators, and the lay public generally concur with the idea that musicians as a group, like other professionals, enjoy high-level intelligence (64). These findings notwithstanding, music psychologists are divided in their opinions. When test scores are used as criteria of musical aptitude, investigators maintain that the relationship between musical and academic intelligence is positive but low. European researchers who employ subjective criteria as evidence of musical aptitude generally,report rather high relationships. Schüssler (76), Haecker and Ziehen (39), and Miller (61), for example, found the relationship between intelligence and musical aptitude (as deduced from musical performance skill) to be noteworthy. Farnsworth (16), Highsmith (43), Hollingsworth (44), Bienstock (1), and Lehman (52), for example, found, at best, only a limited relationship between intelligence and musical aptitude test scores. The latter two even give credence to the belief that, low as it is, the correlation between intelligence and musical achievement is higher than that between intelligence and musical aptitude. Colwell (6), Cooley (7), and Moore (62) tend to support this position. Farnsworth (17) cities evidence of the musical.prowess of some "idiot-savants." Seashore (79), Kwalwasser (50),

Drake (11), and Gordon (34) provide data which further suggests that there is no more than ten to twenty percent common variance between scores on their aptitude tests and general intelligence tests. Gordon found almost identical results when either verbal or nonverbal intelligence test scores were used as criteria.

While it might be gratifying to the musician's ego if the foregoing data were interpreted to support the notion that all intelligent people are not necessarily musical but all musical people are intelligent, we might temper our approval by bearing in mind that creative people are not necessarily highly intelligent. That is, like intelligence and musical aptitude, the correlation between measures of intelligence and creativity (not necessarily musical creativity) has not been found to be so high as originally anticipated by some philosophers.

The reader has probably inferred from the foregoing discussion that the nature of the relationship of intelligence to musical aptitude has in the past been mainly of theoretical interest. Nevertheless, from a practical point of view, music educators must still determine whether or not it is justifiable to identify students for special music instruction according to intelligence scores rather than to demonstrated musical aptitude. It is common procedure for some instrumental music teachers to select the more academically capable students at the fourth- or fifth-grade level to study an instrument. Perhaps it is assumed that because intelligence scores of students are generally available, and because it would take additional time to obtain musical aptitude scores, the sole use of intelligence scores will suffice. Because participation in school music activities often requires additional student time, it is reasoned that brighter students have more time to engage in musical activities in that they complete their academic work with greater ease than students of lesser intelligence. Specifically, intelligent students are said to learn more quickly how to finger an instrument and to read musical notation. As a result of this fallacious selection process, we find a large number of students in instrumental music performance groups who have more technical understanding than musical insight. This may be a primary factor contributing to the alarmingly high performance group "drop-out" rate among high school students. It may also be a factor in the lack of enthusiasm of former high school instrumental musicians for participating in college and community music activities (45). Evidently, many students who have high musical aptitude and who would naturally enjoy the success which would accrue from continued participation in appropriate music activities are not identified to receive instruction. Conversely, many intelligent students who are selected for special music instruction become bored by their intensive association with music activities because they lack the necessary musical aptitude to derive serious enjoyment from their endeavors.

Of even more practical importance to the teacher is the way in which musical aptitude and intelligence, when considered *together,* can identify musically talented students and predict success in musical achievement. Only one recent study (29) deals specifically with this problem, however. Through the use of multiple regression techniques, when both the *Henmon-Nelson Tests of Mental Ability* scores and *MAP* scores of fifth-grade students were employed to predict degree of success in instrumental music, the increase in precision was only negligibly better than when *MAP* was used alone, but significantly better than when only the intelligence test was used. The same findings occurred when *MAP* was used in conjunction with the *Iowa Test of Basic Skills,* an achievement battery. As a matter of fact, when all three tests were used as a group for this purpose, the multiple correlation coefficient, as could be expected, was no higher than that found for any pair of tests of which *MAP* was one.

It is well known that the correlation between scores on intelligence and academic achievement tests is relatively high, almost as high as the reliability of the tests. Unfortunately, however, the correlation between *MAP* scores and musical achievement test scores is comparatively low— approximately the same magnitude (31) as that found between *MAP* scores and academic achievement test scores (34). Obviously, for some reason, students are unable to take full advantage of their potential for musical achievement. Parenthetically, the old wives' tale that musical aptitude and mathematical ability go hand-in-hand lacks objective credibility when *MAP* scores, *Iowa Tests of Basic Skills,* and *Iowa Tests of Education Development* subtests of arithmetic and mathematics, respectively, are used as criteria (34). In both cases, language arts subtests generally show a higher relationship to musical aptitude than do the quantitative subtests.

Interest in learning music, especially as a predictor of musical success, has been almost totally ignored by music psychologists. However, if we accept as criteria of interest in music the degree to which one 1) likes to practice on an instrument, 2) participates in extracurricular music activities, and 3) avails himself of musical instruction during the summer months, we find that the correlation between each one of these variables with *MAP* scores is systematically higher than that found between *MAP* scores and socio-economic status (31). Furthermore, there is a one-to-one relationship between these three variables and *MAP* scores and the three variables and musical achievement test scores (31). What is most striking, however, is that the correlation between *MAP* scores and interest in music is lower than that between *MAP* scores and intelligence test scores, low as the latter relationship is.

From the little evidence we have, we can only assume that one's interest in music does affect his success in music. In keeping with the findings relating to other fields, it appears that interest, though of significant value when combined with aptitude, cannot be considered a practicable substitute for aptitude.

Before dispensing with the topic of psychological characteristics, a few words concerning the personality traits of musicians are in order. Long before the supposed corroborating research of the Pannenborgs (65), Feis (19), and Kretschmer (48) around the turn of the century, it had been assumed that musicians as a group are "emotional" and not "orderly" or "punctual." More positively, these researchers suggested that musicians have extensive artistic and linguistic abilities and that they enjoy social intercourse. The fact that some of the musicians studied in the course of these experiments (either in observational or biographical form) were alleged to be mentally unstable or given to immaturity and hysteria does not mean that all musicians have such characteristics. The claim of these investigators that mathematical ability and intelligence are closely related to musical aptitude suggests that their other findings may have been somewhat in error.

More recently, Garder (23) and Lehman (52) reported that musicianship, as displayed by college and high school students, is related to superior social adjustment. Duda (14), using the *Strong Vocational Interest Blank* and other similar tests, found student teachers in music to have creative imagination and initiative. Cooley's research (7) does not support these contentions, nor does Schleuter's (74), which indicates that there is no common factor which includes both personality traits and characteristics of musical aptitude or musical achievement.

In spite of the paucity of research pertaining to the relationship between personality traits and musical aptitude, common sense dictates that knowledge of this relationship would theoretically have, at best, little value for music educators. Suffice it to say that students with high musical aptitude need to be challenged and that the abilities of low aptitude students must be developed as best one can, their aberrant inclinations of sinistrality, ambidexterity, or purblindness notwithstanding.

Race, Religion, and Nationality

The musical aptitude of various ethnic groups has been of great interest to music psychologists. However, very little data have appeared in the literature during the last thirty years or so, and probably with good reason. Behavioral scientists have found that sociological studies are influenced by the nationality of the subject and by the specific part of the country in which he lives. Furthermore, in studies of this type it is difficult, if not impossible, to categorize certain groups specifically because of the extensive mixing of races, religions, and national origins. The following findings are affected to some degree by these limitations.

Using the Seashore test, Lenoire (53) found Negro children to be superior to whites in rhythm and tonal memory and not inferior on the other measures; Peterson and Lanier (67) report that whites scored higher on all tests but not higher than Negroes on rhythm; Gray and Bingham (37) claim Negroes equaled whites only on the consonance test; and, in marked contradiction, Johnson (46) found no significant difference between the two groups. Peacock (66), however, suggests that the tests favor whites in all categories. Inconsistent results were also evidenced with the Kwalwasser-Dykema battery. Woods and Martin (103) found Negroes to be superior only in rhythm and consonance, while Robinson and Holmes (71) found whites superior in all aspects.

Farnsworth (16), using tests of pitch, consonance, melody, and harmony, found that native-born whites were superior only in melody when compared to native- and foreign-born Orientals. Again, employing the Seashore battery as criteria, Garth and Candor (24) and Garth and Isbell (25) found Mexicans inferior in pitch and rhythm and American Indians superior in time and rhythm. Porter (68) reported that both Orientals and whites, who shared similar environmental characteristics, scored below average on all subtests; Ross (72) found American Indians to be deficient in all respects except time, while Japanese were superior in both time and consonance; and Eells (15) reported that Eskimos scored below average on each of the six subtests.

In investigations of the relationship of musical aptitude to religion and nationality, Sward (91) and Sanderson (73) used both the Seashore and Kwalwasser-Dykema batteries (the former also utilized the Drake *Musical Memory* test). In both studies Jewish students were found to be superior to all others on an overall basis; the order, as reported by Sanderson is Jewish, German, Italian, Negro, and Polish. Negroes scored higher on rhythm than any other group.

In studies in which more recent tests were used as criteria Drake (11) reports no significant differences in scores obtained by Negro and white high school students on his *Musical Memory* subtest or by Negro, white, or Indian students on his *Rhythm* subtest. In the *Musical Aptitude Profile* manual, correlation coefficients representing the relationship of musical aptitude to race and religion are reported that are positive but negligible (34). However, recognizing the restrictive nature of the sample from which this evidence was gathered, Gordon (27) reported supportive data obtained under favorable experimental conditions. In the latter investigation the distribution of *MAP* scores of 658 students enrolled in two predominantly Negro midwestern junior high schools was found to be almost identical to that upon which *MAP* norms are based.

We can only conclude from our information that race, nationality, religion, and sex are not systematically associated with musical aptitude, with the possible specific exception of rhythm aptitude. There are boys and girls who possess varying degrees of musical aptitudes within different ethnic groups. It is reasonable, then, to assume that any person is capable of achieving musical success to the extent his aptitude will allow, regardless of extraneous factors. That culturally disadvantaged students are not fulfilling their potential, however, is evidenced by the recent findings (27) indicating that only eight of fifty-five such students in a given school district who scored above the 90th percentile on *MAP* were in any way involved in school music activities. Social and economic factors related to poor environmental conditions probably exert more influence (both positive and negative) on *musical attainment* than do race or nationality. For example, environmental conditions could easily prevent a musically gifted student who is culturally disadvantaged from achieving success commensurate with his potential. However, his cognizance of the fact that music is generally regarded as one of the fields in which ability is the prime requisite for success could prove to be a highly motivating factor. In view of the difficulties involved in conducting ethnic-aptitude studies, music psychologists might more properly have concerned themselves with investigating the effect of motor ability on various aspects of musical achievement—a topic which for all practical purposes has been ignored in the literature.

SUMMARY

Musical aptitude is comprised of tonal imagery, rhythm imagery, and musical sensitivity. The last includes aesthetic expressive-interpretive qualities. Musical memory of the tonal and rhythm types appears to be largely a measure of musical achievement. Evidence suggests that rhythm imagery is the basis, and musical sensitivity the unifying element, of musical aptitude.

Environmental factors such as socio-economic status and musical training bear little or no relationship to musical aptitude. Nor have race, religion, or nationality been found to affect levels of musical aptitude either positively or negatively. Culturally disadvantaged and advantaged groups may both contain musically talented students. It appears, however, that low socio-economic status impinges on musical achievement.

The correlation between intelligence and musical aptitude test scores is positive but low. Academic achievement test scores correlate somewhat higher with musical aptitude test scores. Musical aptitude test scores predict success in musical achievement significantly better than either intelligence or academic achievement test scores.

Subjective notions notwithstanding, research has not indicated any substantial relationship between musical aptitude and specific personality characteristics.

STUDY GUIDE

1. Explain why musical aptitude is to musical achievement what intelligence is to academic achievement.
2. Why is it so difficult to describe subjectively the components of musical aptitude?
3. Differentiate between the "Gestalt" and "atomistic" theories of musical aptitude test construction in regard to psychological constructs.
4. Explain the difference between musical aptitude preference and nonpreference tests.
5. How does a tonal imagery test differ from tests of pitch discrimination, pitch recognition, and pitch memory?
6. How does a rhythm imagery test differ from tests of time discrimination, rhythm discrimination, and rhythm memory?
7. Outline what you consider to be the components of musical aptitude and defend their construct validity.
8. Offer reasons why musical exposure affects musical aptitude at a very early age but not after age nine or ten.
9. Explain the observed low positive correlation between musical aptitude and intelligence test scores.
10. Suggest reasons why musically creative talent is not necessarily related to academic intelligence.
11. Why might low socio-economic status affect musical achievement and not musical aptitude?
12. Discuss the popular notion that Negroes have higher rhythmic aptitudes than whites; that musicians possess exceptional mathematical ability.

BIBLIOGRAPHY

1. Bienstock, Sylvia, "A Predictive Study of Musical Achievement," *Journal of Genetic Psychology*, LXI (1942), 135–45.

2. Benham, Evelyn, "The Creative Activity: Introspective Experiment in Musical Composition," *British Journal of Psychology*, XX (1929), 59–65.

3. Bentley, Arnold, *Musical Ability in Children and Its Measurement.* New York: October House, Inc., 1966.

4. Bower, Libbie, *A Factor Analysis of Music Tests.* Washington: Catholic University Press, 1945.

5. Burt, Cyril, *Psychological Tests of Educable Capacity.* London: Board of Education, 1924.

6. Colwell, Richard, "An Investigation of Musical Achievement Among Public School Students," *Journal of Educational Research,* LVII (1964), 355–59.

7. Cooley, John, "A Study of the Relation Between Certain Mental and Personality Traits and Ratings of Musical Ability," *Journal of Research in Music Education,* IX (1961), 108–17.

8. Cowell, Henry, "The Process of Musical Creation," *American Journal of Psychology,* XXXVII (1926), 233–36.

9. Cox, C., *Genetic Studies of Genius.* Stanford: Stanford University Press, 1926.

10. Drake, Raleigh, *Drake Musical Aptitude Tests.* Chicago: Science Research Associates, 1954.

11. Drake, Raleigh, *Drake Musical Aptitude Tests Manual.* Chicago: Science Research Associates, 1954, pp. 17, 19, 21.

12. Drake, Raleigh, "Factorial Analysis of Music Tests by the Spearman Tetrad-Difference Technique," *Journal of Musicology,* I (1939), 6–16.

13. Drake, Raleigh, "Four New Tests of Musical Talent," *Journal of Applied Psychology,* XVII (1933), 136–47.

14. Duda, W. B., "The Prediction of Three Major Dimensions of Teacher Behavior for Student Teachers in Music." Unpublished Ed.D. dissertation, University of Illinois, 1961.

15. Eells, Walter, "Musical Ability of the Native Races of Alaska," *Journal of Applied Psychology,* XVII (1933), 67–71.

16. Farnsworth, Paul, "An Historical, Critical, and Experimental Study of the Seashore-Kwalwasser Test Battery," *Genetic Psychology Monograph,* IX (1931), 291–393.

17. Farnsworth, Paul, *The Social Psychology of Music.* New York: Dryden Press, 1958.

18. Faulds, Bruce, *The Perception of Pitch in Music.* Princeton, New Jersey: Educational Testing Service, 1959.

19. Feis, Oswald, *Studien über die Genealogie und Psychologie der Musik.* Wiesbaden: J. F. Bergman, 1910.

20. Flanagan, John, et al., *Project Talent Monograph Series.* Pittsburgh: University of Pittsburgh Press. 1962.

21. Franklin, Erik, *Tonality as a Basis for the Study of Musical Talent.* Göteborg, Sweden: Gumperts Forlag, 1956.

22. Froseth, James, "An Investigation of the Use of Musical Aptitude Profile Scores in the Instruction of Beginning Students in Instrumental Music." Unpublished Ph.D. dissertation, University of Iowa, 1968.

23. Garder, C. E., "Characteristics of Outstanding High School Musicians," *Journal of Research in Music Education,* III (1955), 11–20.

24. Garth, T. R., and E. Candor, "Musical Talent of Mexicans," *American Journal of Psychology,* XLIX (1937), 203–7.

25. Garth, T. R., and S. R. Isbell, "The Musical Talent of Indians," *Music Supervisors Journal,* XV (1929), 85–87.

26. Gaston, E. Thayer, *Test of Musicality.* Lawrence, Kansas: Odell's Instrumental Service, 1957.

27. Gordon, Edwin, "A Comparison of the Performance of Culturally Disadvantaged with That of Culturally Heterogeneous Students on the Musical Aptitude Profile," *Psychology in the Schools,* XV (1967), 260–68.

28. Gordon, Edwin, "An Investigation of the Intercorrelation Among Musical Aptitude Profile and Seashore Measures of Musical Talents Subtests," *Journal of Research in Music Education,* XVII (1969), 263–71.

29. Gordon, Edwin, "A Study of the Efficacy of General Intelligence and Musical Aptitude Tests in Predicting Achievement in Music," *Council for Research in Music Education,* XIII (1968), 40–45.

30. Gordon, Edwin, "A Study to Determine the Effects of Practice and Training on Drake Musical Aptitude Test Scores," *Journal of Research in Music Education,* IV (1961), 63–74.

31. Gordon, Edwin, *A Three-Year Longitudinal Predictive Validity Study of the Musical Aptitude Profile.* Vol. 5 of *Studies in the Psychology of Music.* Iowa City: University of Iowa, 1968.

32. Gordon, Edwin, "Implications for the Use of the Musical Aptitude Profile with College and University Freshman Music Students," *Journal of Research in Music Education,* XV (1967), 32–40.

33. Gordon, Edwin, *Musical Aptitude Profile.* Boston: Houghton Mifflin Company, 1965.

34. Gordon, Edwin, *Musical Aptitude Profile Manual.* Boston: Houghton Mifflin Company, 1965, p. 10.

35. Gordon, Edwin, "The Contribution of Each Musical Aptitude Profile

Subtest to the Overall Validity of the Battery," *Council for Research in Music Education,* XII (1967), 32–36.

36. Gordon, Edwin, "The Use of the Musical Aptitude Profile with Exceptional Children," *Journal of Music Therapy,* V (1968), 37–40.

37. Gray, C. T., and C. W. Bingham, "A Comparison of Certain Phases of Musical Ability in Colored and White School Pupils," *Journal of Educational Psychology,* XX (1929), 501–6.

38. Gross, B., and R. H. Seashore, "Psychological Characteristics of Student and Professional Musical Composers," *Journal of Applied Psychology,* XXV (1941), 159–70.

39. Haecker, V., and T. Ziehen, "Über die Erblichkeit der musikalischen Begabung," *Zeitschrift für Psychologie,* XCVII (1925), 191–214.

40. Hatfield, Warren, "An Investigation of the Diagnostic Validity of MAP with Respect to Instrumental Performance." Unpublished Ph.D. dissertation, University of Iowa, 1967.

41. Heinlein, Christian Paul, "A Brief Discussion of the Nature and Function of Melodic Configuration in Tonal Memory with Critical Reference to the Seashore Tonal Memory Test," *Pedagogical Seminary and Journal of Genetic Psychology,* XXXV (1928), 45–61.

42. Heller, Jack, "The Effects of Formal Training on Wing Musical Intelligence Scores." Unpublished Ph.D. dissertation, University of Iowa, 1962.

43. Highsmith, J. A., "Selecting Musical Talent," *Journal of Applied Psychology,* XIII (1929), 486–93.

44. Hollingsworth, Leta, "Musical Sensitivity of Children Who Score Above 135 I.Q.," *Journal of Educational Psychology,* XVII (1926), 95–109.

45. Horner, V., *Music Education.* Hawthorn, Victoria: Australian Council for Educational Research, 1965.

46. Johnson, G. B., "Musical Talent and the American Negro," *Music Supervisors Journal,* LXXXI (1928), 13, 86.

47. Karlin, J. E., "A Factorial Study of Auditory Function," *Psychometrika,* VII (1942), 251–79.

48. Kretschmer, E., *The Psychology of Men of Genius.* New York: Harcourt Brace Jovanovich, Inc., 1931.

49. Kwalwasser, Jacob, and Peter Dykema, *Kwalwasser-Dykema Music Tests.* New York: Carl Fischer, 1930.

50. Kwalwasser, Jacob, *Exploring the Musical Mind.* New York: Coleman-Ross, 1955.

51. Kwalwasser, Jacob, *Kwalwasser Music Talent Test.* New York: Mills Music Company, 1953.

52. Lehman, Charles, "A Comparative Study of Instrumental Musicians on the Basis of the Otis Intelligence Test, the Kwalwasser-Dykema Music Test and the Minnesota Multiphasic Personality Inventory," *Journal of Educational Research,* XLIV (1950), 57–61.

53. Lenoire, Z., "Measurement of Racial Differences in Certain Mental and Educational Abilities." Unpublished Ph.D. dissertation, University of Iowa, 1925.

54. Lowery, H., "Cadence and Phrase Tests in Music," *British Journal of Psychology,* XVII (1926), 111–18.

55. Lowery, H., "Music Memory," *British Journal of Psychology,* XIX (1929), 397–404.

56. Lowery, H., "On the Integrative Theory of Musical Talent," *Journal of Musicology,* II (1940), 1–14.

57. Lundin, Robert, *An Objective Psychology of Music.* New York: The Ronald Press Company, 1967.

58. McLeish, John, "The Validation of Seashore's Measures of Musical Talent by Factorial Methods," *British Journal of Psychology, Statistical Section,* III (1950), 129–40.

59. Mainwaring, James, "The Assessment of Musical Ability," *British Journal of Educational Psychology,* XVII (1947), 83–96.

60. Manzer, Charles, and Samuel Marowitz, "The Performance of a Group of College Students on the Kwalwasser-Dykema Music Tests," *Journal of Applied Psychology,* XIX (1935), 331–46.

61. Miller, Richard, "Über musikalische Begabung und ihre Beziehung zu Sonstigen Anlagen," *Zeitschrift für Psychologie,* XCVII (1925), 191–214.

62. Moore, Ray, "The Relationship of Intelligence to Creativity," *Journal of Research in Music Education,* XIV (1966), 243–53.

63. Mursell, James, and Mabelle Glenn, *The Psychology of School Music Teaching.* New York: Silver Burdett Company, 1931.

64. Mursell, James, *The Psychology of Music.* New York: W. W. Norton & Company, Inc., 1937.

65. Pannenborg, H. J., and W. A. Pannenborg, "Die Psychologie des Musikers," *Zeitschrift für Psychologie,* LXXIII (1915), 91–136.

66. Peacock, W., "A Comparative Study of Musical Talent in Whites and Negroes and Its Correlation with Intelligence." Unpublished Ph.D. dissertation, Emory University, 1928.

67. Peterson, Joseph, and Lyle Lanier, "Studies in the Comparative Abilities of Whites and Negroes," *Mental Measurement Monographs*, V (1929).

68. Porter, Raymond, *A Study of the Musical Talent of the Chinese Attending Public Schools in Chicago.* Chicago: University of Chicago Press, 1931.

69. Rainbow, Edward, "A Pilot Study to Investigate the Constructs of Musical Aptitude." *Journal of Research in Music Education*, XIII (1965), 3–14.

70. Revesz, Geza, *The Psychology of a Musical Prodigy.* New York: Harcourt Brace Jovanovich, 1925.

71. Robinson, Viola, and Mary Holmes, "A Comparison of Negroes and Whites in Musical Ability." Unpublished Master's thesis, Syracuse University, 1932.

72. Ross, Verne, "Musical Talents of Indian and Japanese Children," *Journal of Juvenile Research*, XX (1936), 133–36.

73. Sanderson, Helen, "Differences in Musical Ability in Children of Different National and Racial Origins," *Journal of Genetic Psychology*, XLII (1933), 100–120.

74. Schleuter, Stanley, *An Investigation of the Interrelation of Personality Traits, Musical Aptitude, and Musical Achievement.* Unpublished Ph.D. dissertation, University of Iowa, 1970.

75. Schoen, Max, *The Psychology of Music.* New York: The Ronald Press Company, 1940.

76. Schüssler, H., "Das unmusikalische Kind," *Zeitschrift für Angewandte Psychologie*, XI (1916), 136–66.

77. Seashore, C. E., Don Lewis, and Joseph Saetveit, *Seashore Measures of Musical Talents.* New York: Psychological Corporation, 1956.

78. Seashore, C. E., Don Lewis, and Joseph Saetveit, *Seashore Measures of Musical Talents Manual.* New York: Psychological Corporation, 1956, p. 4.

79. Seashore, C. E. *Psychology of Music.* New York: McGraw-Hill Book Company, 1938, p. 129.

80. Seashore, C.E., *Seashore Measures of Musical Talent.* New York: Columbia Phonograph Company, 1919.

81. Seashore, C. E., *Seashore Measures of Musical Talent Manual.* New York: Columbia Phonograph Company. 1919.

82. Semeonoff, B., "A New Approach to the Testing of Musical Ability," *British Journal of Psychology*, XXX (1940), 326–40.

83. Shuter, Rosamund, *The Psychology of Musical Ability.* London: Methuen & Co. Ltd., 1968.

84. Squires, P. C., "The Creative Psychology of Carl Maria von Weber," *Character and Personality*, VI (1938), 203–17.

85. Squires, P. C., "The Creative Psychology of Cesar Franck," *Character and Personality*, VII (1938), 41–49.

86. Squires, P. C., "The Creative Psychology of Chopin," *Journal of Musicology*, II (1940), 27–37.

87. Stanton, Hazel, and Wilhelmine Koerth, *Musical Capacity Measures in Adults Repeated After Musical Education*. Studies on the Aims and Progress of Research. Iowa City: University of Iowa, 1933.

88. Stanton, Hazel, *Measurement of Musical Talent: The Eastman Experiment*. Studies in the Psychology of Music. Iowa City: University of Iowa, 1935.

89. Streep, Rosalind, "A Comparison of White and Negro Children in Rhythm and Consonance," *Journal of Applied Psychology*, XV (1931), 53–71.

90. Stumpf, Carl, "Akustische Versuche mit Pepito Areola," *Zeitschrift fur Experimentelle und Angewandte Psychologie*, II (1909), 1–11.

91. Sward, K., "Jewish Musicality in America," *Journal of Applied Psychology*, XVII (1933), 675–712.

92. Tilson, Lowell, "A Study of the Prognostic Value of the Tilson-Gretsch Test for Musical Aptitude," *Teachers College Journal*, XII (1941), 110–112.

93. Vernon, P. E., "Auditory Perception: The Evolutionary Approach," *British Journal of Psychology*, XXV (1935), 265–81.

94. Vernon, P. E., "Auditory Perception: The Gestalt Approach," *British Journal of Psychology*, XXV (1934), 123–39.

95. Vernon, P. E., "Method in Music Psychology," *American Journal of Psychology*, XLII (1930), 127–34.

96. Vernon, P. E., "The Personality of the Composer." *Music and Letters*, XI (1930), 38–48.

97. Vernon, P. E., *The Structure of Human Abilities*. New York: John Wiley & Sons, Inc., 1950.

98. Whitley, Mary, "A Comparison of the Seashore and Kwalwasser-Dykema Music Tests," *Teachers College Record*, XXXIII (1932), 731–51.

99. Wing, Herbert, "A Factorial Study of Music Tests," *British Journal of Psychology*, XXXI (1941), 341–55.

100. Wing, Herbert, "A Revision of the Wing Musical Aptitude Tests," *Journal of Research in Music Education*, X (1962), 39–46.

101. Wing, Herbert, *Standardised Tests of Musical Intelligence*. Sheffield, England: City of Sheffield Training College, 1958.

102. Wing, Herbert, "Tests of Musical Ability and Appreciation," *British Journal of Educational Psychology, Monograph Supplement,* VIII (1948), 1–88.

103. Woods, R., and L. Martin, "Testing in Musical Education," *Education and Psychological Measurement,* III (1943), 29–42.

104. Wyatt, Ruth, "Improvability of Pitch Discrimination," *Psychological Monographs,* LVIII (1945), 1–58.

CHAPTER
THREE

the evaluation
of musical aptitude

A test author would be remiss if he described a musical aptitude test he developed simply as ". . . a valid test of musical aptitude." There is no way for him to be sure that his educated opinion regarding the description of musical aptitude, as represented by the psychological constructs upon which the test is based, is valid. Only when positive results of various types of empirical validity investigations of his test are available can a test author offer objective *support* for his initial subjective opinion. And, a test cannot just be declared valid. It must be shown to be valid for one or more specific purposes. That is, a test is valid only when it has been demonstrated that it is valid *for something*.

After the subject matter of the test items is decided upon (construct validity) and the mechanical design of the test, including the manner in which subjects will give answers to items (process validity), is determined, a test constructor becomes interested in aspects of the reliability (score stability) and the efficiency (time requirements) of the measures. The first step in establishing the reliability of the test is to examine the quality of each test item with regard to its difficulty level (the number of students who successfully answer the item) and its discriminative value (how well the item differentiates between high- and low-scoring students). Then, when the test is refined through these item analysis techniques, actual test reliability is estimated through procedures such as split-halves, test-retest, and/or parallel forms methods. The primary reason that reliability merits such important consideration is that unless results for each student on the same or nearly identical measures are consistent (highly correlated), the possibility of determining the relationship of those results to an outside criterion (validity) will be limited. Stated another way, unless musical aptitude test results agree with themselves, they cannot adequately demonstrate any type of relationship to another factor such as musical achievement. In this sense, reliability is thought of as a necessary but not sufficient condition for establishing statistical validity of a test. Likewise, the nature of the interrelationship (intercorrelation) among subtests that constitute a battery provides evidence of validity in that if two subtests, regardless of their titles, are measuring nearly the same factor and thus are found to be highly intercorrelated, the construct validity of the battery becomes suspect to the extent that one of the subtests might rightfully be eliminated.

At the point when reliability and intercorrelation information substantiate the orientation of the test author, the relationship of test scores to other factors (criterion-related validity) is investigated. For example, it is necessary for musical aptitude test scores to demonstrate a definite concurrent relationship to musical achievement. While it is true that a high correlation between the two criteria *might suggest* that the aptitude test is an achievement measure (because a correlation coefficient only describes the extent of a relationship but not the causation of that relationship), it would be of more concern to find little or no correlation between the two because logic dictates such a positive relationship. The cause of a relationship must be investigated through other procedures in the process of further development of the test. However, further preliminary validity evidence dealing with the concurrent relationship of musical aptitude scores to factors such as intelligence that should have little association with the test must also be obtained. If in this case a low correlation is found, we have what might be called indirect evidence of validity. It would be encouraging to know that the test is not necessarily measuring a trait it was not designed to measure.

As stated, evidence of favorable criterion-related validity of a test, though insufficient in and of itself, actually functions in the development of the battery. Without this type of initial objective validity, it would not be wise to engage in more sophisticated investigations of the experimental validity of a test. With initial objective validity demonstrated, the test developer knows that he is working in a positive direction and that studies of the predictive and diagnostic uses of the test battery, which, in part, help clarify the nature of the causative factor of the concurrent relationship found in criterion-related validity studies, are warranted.

THE USES OF A MUSICAL APTITUDE TEST

In essence, there are two *primary* purposes for using a musical aptitude test: 1) to evaluate students' overall musical aptitude, and 2) to diagnose students' specific musical strengths and weaknesses, as compared to *themselves* (idiographically) and to their peers (normatively) who are enrolled in music classes and in music performance groups.

In an attempt to conceptualize these unique functions of a standardized musical aptitude test, the reader is asked to recall *only* ten students with whom he is intimately acquainted and rank them subjectively in order according to their tonal, rhythmic, and expressive musical aptitudes, and then according to their overall musical aptitude. Because the typical teacher will find this a difficult task, the value of an objective musical aptitude test for comparing hundreds of students according to seven or more separate musical aptitudes should become immediately apparent. Of course, a teacher can construct his own aptitude measure. But, aside from the difficulty of establishing adequate test content not substantially confounded with musical achievement, or of obtaining stability in evaluation, expense in time and finances almost precludes validating a teacher-made aptitude tool for even a single purpose. Further, with subjective measures or an unstandardized test, the provision of national norms becomes impossible.

When a musical aptitude battery is to be used for identifying students who can profit most from and contribute most to special music activities, the longitudinal predictive validity of the standardized test should be investigated. That is, the pretraining composite test score (preferably derived from appropriately weighted subtest scores) should be known to predict relative success on various musical achievement criteria after sufficient training has taken place.

In order to diagnose the idiographic and normative musical strengths and weaknesses of students so that their individual musical needs may be met, the subtests that constitute the musical aptitude battery should be relatively unrelated to each other, but they should represent important dimensions of musical aptitude which are related to actual specific musical behaviors. That is, each subtest should have high reliability and only comparatively low intercorrelation with every other subtest in the battery (certainly the intercorrelation between any two subtests should not be any higher, and hopefully much lower, than the reliability of either of the subtests), and each subtest should be related to at least one important type of musical behavior. For a battery with established diagnostic validity, the accompanying test manual should indicate the relationships of students' high and low subtest scores, as indicated by their musical aptitude profiles, to specific musical behaviors.

A well-constructed musical aptitude test may also be used for such purposes as evaluating the collective potential of groups of students within the same school or school system and for educational and vocational guidance. In addition, individual teachers continually develop distinctive uses for aptitude test results that have relevance to their own music programs and specific needs.

As previously indicated, musical aptitude is a product of the interaction of innate potential and early environmental influences, and therefore, it does not become relatively stable until about fourth-grade level. Because of fluctuation of aptitude levels in early childhood and the present lack of an appropriate musical aptitude test for very young children, it is advisable for teachers to make periodic subjective evaluations of the musical aptitude and achievement of very young children. As a result of early childhood musical training, students may be expected to have adequately developed their potential by the age of nine or ten; at this point their actual levels of musical aptitude may be evaluated objectively through the use of a standardized test.

ESSENTIALS OF A MUSICAL APTITUDE TEST

In evaluating a musical aptitude test, both reliability and validity data must be examined. Validity, however, is the principal factor, for although a test may be reliable, it may lack substantial validity. Conversely, a test cannot demonstrate satisfactory validity unless it is reliable. Reliability is a necessary but not sufficient condition for validity because, theoretically, the validity coefficient of a test can be no higher, and in most cases will be considerably lower, than the square root of the reliability coefficient reported for that test.

Various types of information should be reported in a musical aptitude test battery manual. Test means, standard deviations, reliability coefficients, intercorrelation coefficients, and validity should be presented. Procedures used in the standardization program and methods of score conversions should be explained. All of these data are useful in evaluating the quality and value of a musical aptitude battery.

Test means, standard deviations, intercorrelation coefficients, reliability coefficients, and norms should be reported for each subtest, total test, and composite score according to groups for whom the test was designed. In general, these statistics are best reported for specific school grades. Test means should be approximately between a chance score (the raw score equal to the number of items divided by the number of alternative responses for each item) and the total possible score. If this theoretical mean is too high or too low, it is possible that the test is too easy or too difficult, respectively, for students in the specified grade. Ideally, the total possible score should approximate three standard deviations above the reported mean, and a chance score should approximate three standard deviations below the reported mean. Subtest reliability coefficients should be at least .70, total tests at least .80, and the composite score .90 and above. Intercorrelation coefficients are most desirable when they lie near .00, and they become suspect as they approach or exceed the reliability of the tests.

The construct validity of the test should be considered before its experimental validity is evaluated. That is to say, unless the orientation of the test user is in accordance with the psychological constructs embodied in the test, the teacher will have little or no confidence in the results of the test even if it demonstrates extraordinary experimental validity. In this sense, construct validity has relevance to the individual test user and thus is primarily subjective. It should be recognized, however, that test intercorrelation and reliability coefficients lend objectivity to the assessment of the construct validity of a musical aptitude test. If the test is not highly reliable it may be assumed that what the test author theorizes to be musical aptitude is not being appropriately measured or that it does not really exist. Moreover, if the subtest intercorrelation coefficients are exceedingly high, almost as high as the reliabilities of the subtests, it is possible that what the test author considers to be several separate dimensions of musical aptitude actually constitute only, one musical aptitude.

After the teacher finds the construct validity of the tests acceptable, statistical evidence of the longitudinal predictive validity and of the diagnostic validity of the battery should be examined. (As previously indicated, the criterion-related validity of a musical aptitude test is mainly of theoretical interest.) Coefficients associated with test validity can be expected to be lower than the reliability coefficients reported for the tests, but they should have predictive validity of at least .30 to be of practical use in identifying talented students. For example, the *MAP* composite score reliability for elementary school students is above .90 and the longitudinal validity of the test for predicting success in instrumental music over a three-year period is reported in the test manual to be .75. By squaring the validity coefficient it can be determined that over fifty percent of the variability in instrumental music achievement among students is related to their musical aptitude and that somewhat less than fifty percent of the variability in instrumental music achievement among students is related to factors other than musical aptitude. To this extent the *MAP* composite score can be expected to be of practical use in identifying musically talented students, before they are given instruction, who will benefit most from instrumental music training.

Diagnostic validity coefficients are generally lower than predictive validity coefficients. In the case of the latter, the composite test score is used. In the case of the former, subtest scores are used. Composite tests, primarily because they are longer, are usually more reliable and therefore can be expected to demonstrate higher validity. To be of practical diagnostic value each subtest score should correlate about .30 with one or more specific musical behaviors.

A raw score on a test indicates the number of items a student answers correctly. If one student earns a raw score of 20 and another a raw score of 25, the only fact that can be discerned is that the second scored five points higher than the first. Whether 25 is twice as good or three times as good as 20 can most efficiently be determined when raw scores are converted to percentile ranks. For example, a raw score of 20 may be found to equal a percentile rank of 10 and a raw score of 25 a percentile rank of 20; or it may be that a raw score of 20 may equal a percentile rank of 30 and a raw score of 25 a percentile rank of 90.

The author should report in the test manual not only the percentile rank norms for a battery of musical aptitude tests but also standard score conversions. This is true because subtests in the battery will generally differ in raw score means and standard deviations. In order for each subtest in the battery to contribute equally to the composite score, each must be statistically given the same mean and standard deviation. For example, all of the seven subtests which comprise *MAP* have different raw score means and standard deviations. Therefore, in order to provide an equally weighted composite score, raw scores are converted to standard scores so that each subtest has a mean of 50 and a standard deviation of 10.

Finally, the procedures used in standardizing a musical aptitude test should be described in the test manual. The manner in which the test was administered and the various groups to whom it was given should be reported in detail. From such information the test user can administer the test in similar fashion to insure comparability of norms. More importantly, he can accurately interpret the meaning of the norms.

SUMMARY

Musical aptitude is best evaluated in objective fashion through the use of a well-developed musical aptitude test battery. The two primary purposes of a musical aptitude test battery are: 1) to identify musically talented students who can profit most from and contribute most to school music activities, and 2) to diagnose individual students' specific musical strengths and weaknesses.

The most important aspect of a musical aptitude test battery is its validity. To be of practical value, a battery must be shown to be valid for one or more purposes. The accompanying test manual should include test means, standard deviations, reliability coefficients, intercorrelation coefficients, and validity data. Test standardization procedures also should be presented and the nature of the norms explained.

STUDY GUIDE

1. Differentiate between test reliability and test validity.
2. Explain why, all things being equal, longer tests are more reliable than shorter tests.
3. How does test reliability affect test validity?
4. Identify and explain the differences among various types of test validity.
5. Explain the difference between objective and subjective test validity.
6. What purposes can a well-developed musical aptitude test battery serve that a musical "talent" test cannot?
7. What is the function of test intercorrelation data?
8. Describe how you would validate a musical aptitude test battery if you were to construct one.
9. What is the difference between score conversions and test norms?
10. What factors would you control if you were to standardize a musical aptitude test battery?

BIBLIOGRAPHY

1. Blommers, Paul, and E. F. Lindquist, *Elementary Statistical Methods in Psychology and Education*. Boston: Houghton Mifflin Company, 1960.

2. Buros, Oscar, *The Sixth Mental Measurements Yearbook*. Highland Park, N.J.: The Gryphon Press, 1965.

3. Farnsworth, Charles, *Short Studies in Musical Psychology*. London: Oxford University Press, 1930.

4. French, John, and William Michael et al., *Standards for Educational and*

Psychological Tests and Manuals. Washington: American Psychological Association, Inc., 1966.

5. Gulliksen, Harold, *Theory of Mental Tests*. New York: John Wiley & Sons, Inc., 1961.

6. Kwalwasser, Jacob, *Tests and Measurements in Music*. Boston: C. C. Birchard Co., 1927.

7. Lehman, Paul, *Tests and Measurements in Music*. Englewood Cliffs: Prentice-Hall, Inc., 1968.

8. Lindquist E. F. et al., *Educational Measurement*. Washington: American Council on Education, 1951.

9. Lyman, Howard, *Test Scores and What They Mean*. Englewood Cliffs: Prentice-Hall, Inc., 1963.

10. Pinkerton, F., "Talent Tests and Their Application to the Public School Instrument Music Program," *Journal of Research in Music Education,* X (1963), 75–80.

11. Swisher, Walter, *Psychology for the Music Teacher*. Boston: Oliver Ditson Company, 1927.

12. Teplov, B. M., *Psychologie des Aptitudes Musicales*. Paris: Presses Universitaires de France, 1966.

13. Thorndike, Robert, and Elizabeth Hagen, *Measurement and Evaluation in Psychology and Education*. New York: John Wiley & Sons, Inc., 1969.

14. Whybrew, William, *Measurement and Evaluation in Music*. Dubuque, Iowa: William C. Brown Company, Publishers, 1962.

GLOSSARY FOR PART ONE

Achievement—What a student has learned
Aptitude—A student's potential for learning
Atomistic Theory—The theory that aptitude is comprised of multiple capacities
Battery of Tests—A set of subtests designed as a unit and to be administered as a group
Chance Score—A score obtained by guessing answers
Composite Score—A total score for all subtests of a test battery
Construct Validity—The degree to which a user of the test believes the test to be an accurate measure of a trait
Content Validity—The degree to which test items reflect understandings that the test was designed to measure
Correlation—The relationship between variables

Correlation Coefficient—An index which indicates the degree of relationship between variables; a perfect positive relationship $= +1.00$, no relationship $= 0.00$, and a perfect negative relationship $= -1.00$.

Criterion-Related Validity—The correlation between test scores and a criterion value obtained about the same time

Diagnostic Validity—The correlation between individual subtest scores and specific musical behaviors

Empirical Validity—Validity data based on objective evidence from actual studies

Factor Analysis—A set of procedures for analyzing complex relationships among a group of variables. Common, group, and/or unique factors may be determined.

Gestalt Theory—The theory that aptitude is comprised of only one general capacity

Idiographic Differences—The differences between one student's scores on various subtests in a battery

Intercorrelation—The correlation between any two subtests in a battery

Item Analysis—The study of the statistical properties of test items

Item Difficulty—The percent of students who answer a test item *correctly*

Item Discrimination—A comparison of the percentage of more capable and less capable students who answer a test item correctly

Multiple Regression—A technique for estimating the relationship of a group of variables to a single variable, in contrast to the relationship of a single variable to one other variable

Normal Distribution—A symmetrical bel-shaped curve with a majority of cases being in the middle (average), fewer in the shoulders (above and below average), and very few in the tails (exceptional)

Normative Differences—The differences between various students' scores on the same test

Norms—Frames of references for interpreting test scores

Omnibus Theory—The Gestalt Theory of the composition of musical aptitude

Parallel Test Forms—Equivalent forms of the same test sometimes used for estimating the reliability of a test

Percentile Rank—The percentage of students who score below a given arithmetical point

Predictive Validity—The correlation between a pretraining test score and a criterion value obtained after a period of training

Psychological Construct—An aspect of a theory of the nature of musical aptitude and how it is best tested

Random Sample—A sample of cases drawn from a population in such a way that every member of the population has an equal chance of being selected

Raw Score—A score equal to the number of items answered correctly on a test

Reliability—The stability or consistency of scores on a test

Reliability Coefficient—A correlation coefficient that represents the relationship between two sets of scores on a test, a relationship reflecting the stability or consistency (reliability) of test scores

Score Distribution—The division of all possible scores on a test among students

Split-Halves Reliability—An estimate of reliability determined by dividing one test into two halves and estimating test reliability through the use of the Spearman-Brown Prophecy Formula

Standard Deviation—A measure of variability of scores in a group

Standard Score—A score expressed in standard deviations above or below a mean

Standardized Test—A published test which reports norms, directions for administration, and statistical data in an accompanying manual

Statistical Significance—The degree to which observed facts cannot be attributed to chance

Stratified Sample—A sample of cases drawn from a population in such a way that members of every segment of the population are proportionately represented

Subtest—One of the tests in a battery

Test-Retest Reliability—An estimate of reliability determined by administering the same test on two different occasions

Theoretical Mean—The score midway between a chance score and the total possible score

Total Test—Two or more subtests in a battery which are particularly related by their content

Validity—A general concept relating to the quality of a test.

Validity Coefficient—A correlation coefficient which represents the relationship between test scores and a criterion value

Variability—The extent to which scores in a set deviate from the mean

PART TWO

musical achievement

CHAPTER FOUR

the application of current learning theories to music education

LEARNING THEORIES

Gagné (5), in his discussion of the conditions of learning, outlines eight different types of learning which encompass both Gestalt and association theory. The types are arranged in hierarchical order, from simple perceptual learning to complex conceptual learning. Gagné titles the types as follows:

1. Signal Learning
2. Stimulus-Response Learning
3. Chaining
4. Verbal Association
5. Multiple-Discrimination Learning
6. Concept Learning
7. Principle Learning
8. Problem Solving

These eight general types of learning might best be understood as they apply to musical learning. Signal learning represents simple perception of sound. As one begins to recognize sound as musical sound, a response is generated, the sound being the stimulus and the musical recognition which it elicits from the listener, the response. Stimulus-response learning becomes more complex as one response becomes a stimulus for another response until a series of stimuli and responses takes place. This chaining reaction in musical learning occurs, for example, when the musical recognition of a tone (or tones) that is heard (a response) promotes the expectation (now a stimulus) of hearing another tone (or tones). Chaining is largely a matter of continuous conditioned anticipations. Verbal association takes place when spoken or written descriptions— such as the names of lines and spaces, the time value names of notes, and the names of key and meter signatures—are used to identify responses.

These first four types of learning as described by Gagné are basically perceptual. They are what Woodruff (13) refers to as "input" in the sense that a student "takes in" what he is taught in predominantly rote fashion. Piaget (12) also makes provision for these four types in his description of the first three stages of learning, which are 1) Sensory-Motor Intelligence (age 0 to 2), Preoperational Representation (age 2 to 7), and Concrete Operations (age 7 to 11). In these stages the learner perceptualizes a dominant aspect of music—what Piaget refers to as "centration."

The final four types of learning depicted by Gagné represent comparatively complex types because they are basically conceptual. Woodruff would describe these methods of learning as "output" because through transfer and generalization one thinks for himself, "learns by learning," and creates new or unique ideas. Piaget suggests that these latter types of learning take place during the fourth and final developmental learning stage, Formal Operation (age 11 to 15). "Conservation," as characterized by Piaget, takes place during these stages: "centration" is reversed and compensated for, providing the basis for the conceptual learning process.

Multiple-Discrimination learning, the most fundamental of the conceptual types, takes place as one develops, for example, the ability to differentiate aurally or symbolically between major and minor tonality, duple and triple meter, and two- and three-part form, or between progressive jazz and rock and roll music styles. Concept learning is the ability to transfer and generalize multiple discrimination understandings to unfamiliar music. The mode, meter, form, or style of a new piece of music is recognized by comparison with similar features in familiar music. Principle learning is best described as an understanding of the theoretical nature, for example, of major and minor tonality through the study of intervalic relationships; of duple and triple meter as they relate to note values; of sonata form as it incorporates an exposition, development section, and a recapitulation; or of the underlying rhythmic interpretation of progressive jazz and rock and roll. Finally, as Gagné has more recently suggested, problem-solving learning is basically the same as principle learning; both form the basis for creative endeavors.

TEACHING PRINCIPLES

In music education, as in other disciplines, emphasis is generally put upon the first four types of learning outlined by Gagné. As a result students develop perceptual understanding about music predominantly by rote and rarely engage in conceptual pursuits. This is not because music does not lend itself to conceptual learning but probably because teachers lack the necessary expertise. In the following statement Ausubel (1) at least indirectly corroborates this point of view by explaining the dependency of conceptual learning on appropriate teaching procedures:

> "The distinctive features of a cognitive learning theory as a theory of how learning takes place . . . are that it both a) deals primarily with meaningful as opposed to rote learning and b) emphasizes the salient role of the learner's existing structure of knowledge in defining the conditions, determinants, and outcomes of the acquisition and retention of knowledge."

Without understanding these factors, it is difficult for teachers to direct students in conceptual learning. Teaching procedures which are appropriate for conceptual learning must reflect the idea that, as Ausubel states it (1), "Meaningful learning involves the acquisition of new meanings, and new meanings, conversely, are the products of meaningful learning."

Bruner (3) stresses the teacher's role in encouraging students to go beyond perceptual learning to conceptual learning when he concludes, "Whether the student knows the formal names of these operations is less important for transfer than whether he is able to use them." In this context, knowing that a major triad is constructed by superimposing two thirds is less important than being able to recognize a major triad when it is heard or knowing when it is appropriate to use a major triad in improvising. In order to develop conceptual learning among students, the teacher must be aware of the importance of appropriately structuring subject matter, of providing for readiness for learning, and of motivating students to learn. The extent to which a teacher makes provision for learning readiness will decide the adequacy of the structure of the subject matter the student is expected to learn. Bruner most aptly demonstrates this idea by suggesting that ". . . the foundation of any subject may be taught to anybody at any age in some form." When Bruner refers to ". . . the spiral curriculum that turns back on itself at higher levels . . . ," he is suggesting that understanding acquired through perceptual learning becomes crystallized when it is systematically developed through conceptual learning. Direction for structuring subject matter is given a logical basis through recognition of the fact that perceptual learning represents the readiness for conceptual learning—that is, perceptual learning provides the background and motivation for conceptual learning. In the following statement Bruner conveys the singular importance of conceptual learning to the overall educational process:

> "Virtually all the evidence of the last two decades on the nature of learning and transfer has indicated that . . . it is indeed a fact that massive general transfer can be achieved by appropriate learning, even to the degree that learning properly under optimum conditions leads one to 'learn how to learn.' "

PURPOSE AND OBJECTIVES OF MUSIC EDUCATION

From our analysis of current learning theory, it appears that the process of developing music appreciation has educational significance when it provides for an *understanding* of music and not necessarily for a *love* for music. The better something is understood the greater are the chances that it will be liked. However, it is quite conceivable that something can be well understood but not necessarily liked. The general purpose of music education, then, should be to teach for musical understanding—that is, to help students conceptualize the elements of music so that they may intelligently decide for themselves how music can best satisfy their needs. Through this process students are not told that specific music is either "good" or "bad." Rather, they are guided in learning to discriminate qualities of the many types of music to which they listen.

Music, like spoken language, is comprised of complex sound. In fact, music is even more complex because not only is it expressive and inflective but its rhythm is disciplined and its tonal elements extensive. A human being acquires broad musical meaning from musical sound because he is able to perceive and then organize and conceptualize what he hears. If he is unable to organize and conceptualize what he perceives, for all intents and purposes he hears a mass of unintelligible noise. Because music is an aural art, one must first acquire aural perception and kinesthetic reaction in order to develop musical understanding in a conceptual sense.* Even in regard to verbal association learning, Lowell Mason's pronouncement "sound before sign" is as valid today as it was many years ago. That is, "sound" must be taught before "sign" can be given meaning.

Basically we organize and conceptualize what we hear as musical sound in two ways, tonally and rhythmically. To the degree to which we are able to organize these two elements and conceptualize their interaction, we develop aesthetic response to musical expression. We give meaning to the tonal elements through our aural sense of tonality and to the rhythmic elements through our kinesthetic sense of meter. As a general parallel, when we listen to someone speak, we are able to keep in mind what he is saying and to anticipate what he might say by giving meaning to his preceding words which form the basis of continuous thought. We are able to remember what has been said because we reexperience the familiar organization of familiar words based on the underlying logic of thought. Phrases combine into complete thoughts, and the more we hear, the more we are sure of what is being said and the more we can generally anticipate what will be said. If the words used are unfamiliar (or if all we hear is unintelligible noise), we are unable to remember, analyze, and synthesize as we listen, and what we hear has little meaning for us (8, 9).

So it is with musical sound. Organization of tonal elements is dependent on the extent of our aural familiarity with major, minor, and the unusual modal tonalities. We hear one or possibly more of these tonalities objectively (that is, we continuously perceive an established resting tone) as we listen to and perform music. Using a sense of tonality as the basis for remembering and organizing melodic contour and harmonic function, we conceptualize what we have heard and anticipate what might be heard. Because nontonal music is unfamiliar to us, it may be that each individual subjectively identifies a resting tone by contrasting nontonal music with music based on a traditional mode. Once we objectively agree on the resting tone in nontonal music, that music becomes tonal by definition.

When we consider rhythmic elements, we find that music basically moves in either two's or three's, or combinations thereof. As a result, meter, as it interacts with tempo in a polyrhythmic sense, provides the kinesthetic basis by which we remember, organize, conceptualize, and anticipate melodic and harmonic rhythm. Supposedly, the uninitiated mind subjectively confers meaning on unusual meter by contrasting it to duple and triple meter. Thus, we may say that both meter and tonality provide the underlying logic upon which musical meaning is superimposed.

Musical understanding gives rise to musical sensitivity caused by

---

* It must be recognized that kinesthetic reaction is activated through aural perception.

tension and relaxation. According to Meyer's (9, 10) explanation of information theory, when we hear what we expect, we relax; when we do not hear it, we become tense as we search for new expectations. The reason many of us derive little satisfaction from contemporary music is that we lack a familiar perceptual basis (which comes from experience with the new) for conceptualizing what we hear.

As emphasized in Part One of this book, music imagery constitutes musical aptitude. Each individual's ability to perceive, remember, organize, conceptualize, and anticipate tonal and rhythmic elements is dependent on his tonal and rhythmic imagery (aptitude). Thus, music teachers should not expect all students in a class to achieve equally in music. So often an entire music class is taught as if it really consisted of only one student of average ability. The fact is that every class includes students with vastly different levels of musical aptitude (6).

Simply stated, then, the overall objective of music education is to provide for the idiographic and normative differences among students, as evidenced from their musical aptitudes. When these differences are observed and appropriate teaching takes place, the deficiencies of less musical students are compensated for, while at the same time students with high aptitude are challenged. In this way, specific behavioral objectives can be efficiently identified and the conceptual type of musical achievement, a natural consequence of the attainment of these objectives, is effected. Not only are more gifted students encouraged to enter the profession of music or to follow music as a meaningful avocation, but perhaps even more importantly, less gifted students are genuinely helped to make the most of and enjoy whatever aptitude they possess. A prime role of music education is to make musical culture understandable to the masses, half of whom, by definition, have below average musical aptitude.

What we now might ask is how the overall objective of music education can be accomplished. The answer of course, is to identify specific behavioral objectives, as suggested by Mager (7), and then determine specifically how students learn music—the basic topics of the following chapters.

SUMMARY

Learning types are divided into two general classifications: perceptual and conceptual. The conceptual types of learning are of a higher order. Generalization and transfer best characterize conceptual learning, whereas simple sound reception and memorization are indicative of perceptual learning.

An understanding of current learning theory provides a basis for defining and clarifying the differences among the purpose of music education, the objectives of music education, learning processes which are most conducive to music education, and teaching principles which complement techniques appropriate to learning music.

Because students infer musical meaning from musical sound by being able to remember, organize, and conceptualize what they perceive, the general purpose of music education should be to teach students to understand the music they hear. The overall objective of music education, then, must be to consider students' individual musical needs and abilities, concomitant to identifying and establishing specific behavioral objectives. The purpose and objectives of music education are best effected through an understanding of how students learn music and by adhering to teaching principles that interact with and enhance the musical learning process.

STUDY GUIDE

1. Differentiate between perceptual and conceptual types of learning as they apply to music education.
2. Explain why instruction in music education over the years has emphasized perceptual learning.
3. Why must instruction in music education go beyond verbal association learning?
4. Why should music educators become increasingly concerned with conceptual learning approaches?
5. Relate the principles of information theory to learning music.
6. Explain the relationship of types of learning to teaching principles.
7. Define the nature of a behavioral objective.
8. Why do a sense of tonality and a feeling for meter provide the underlying logic through which music is given meaning?
9. How can knowledge of students' musical aptitude levels contribute to effective instruction in music education?
10. Why is the purpose of music education different from the objectives of music education?

BIBLIOGRAPHY

1. Ausubel, David, "A Cognitive Theory of School Learning," *Psychology in the Schools*, VI (1969), pp. 3, 4, 331–35.

2. Ausubel, David, *The Psychology of Meaningful Verbal Learning*. New York: Grune & Stratton, Inc., 1963.

3. Bruner, Jerome S., *The Process of Education.* Cambridge: Harvard University Press, 1961, pp. 6, 8, 12, 13.

4. Dittemore, Edgar, *"An Investigation of Some Musical Capabilities of Elementary School Children." Studies in the Psychology of Music,* VI (1970), 1–44.

5. Gagne, Robert, *The Conditions of Learning.* New York: Holt, Rinehart and Winston, Inc., 1965.

6. Gordon, Edwin, *Musical Aptitude Profile Manual.* Boston: Houghton Mifflin Company, 1965.

7. Mager, Robert, *Preparing Instructional Objectives.* Palo Alto: Fearon Publishers, 1962.

8. Mainwaring, James, "Psychological Factors in the Teaching of Music," *British Journal of Education Psychology,* XXI (1951), 105–21, 199–213.

9. Meyer, Leonard, *Emotion and Meaning in Music.* Chicago: University of Chicago Press, 1956.

10. Meyer, Leonard, *Music, the Arts, and Ideas.* Chicago: University of Chicago Press, 1967.

11. Nye, Robert, *Music for Elementary School Children.* Washington: Center for Applied Research in Education, 1963.

12. Piaget, Jean, *Construction of Reality in the Child.* New York: Basic Books, 1954.

13. Woodruff, Asahel, *Basic Concepts of Teaching.* San Francisco: Chandler Publishing Co., 1960.

14. Zimmerman, Marilyn, "Musical Concept Formation: A Review of the Research Literature," *Colorado Journal of Research in Music Education,* IV (1968), 1–4.

CHAPTER FIVE

rhythmic learning

It is logical that a person who can speak but cannot read or write his native language can have only limited understanding of history and literature. However, the person who can read and write his native language can not only convey his ideas to others in a permanent form, but may enjoy the rich and boundless experiences of his ancestors and contemporaries, whether near or far, living or dead. When a person is literate in his native language, he can better learn to appreciate that language because he is able to satisfy his individual needs. He can emphasize and study in depth what he chooses, at his own pace, and at his leisure. Likewise, as a person progresses in music from simple rote singing and sensuous listening to the development of music literacy, he will systematically learn to understand music because he will more efficiently conceptualize complex aspects of musical sound and be able to study, create, and perform independently.

It might seem paradoxical that musical understanding generates musical enjoyment, while at the same time musical enjoyment provides the basis for musical understanding. The more a person knows about music, the more he is able to enjoy it, and the more he enjoys music, the more he is able to learn about it. To become truly musically literate, one must first acquire basic enjoyment and understanding of music in the form of developed musical imagery—that is, aural perception and kinesthetic reaction. In this sense, learning to read and write music may be compared to the ability to read and write the spoken word. In order to be read, words must first have meaning. As Ohmann (25) indicates, oral vocabulary is then associated with written words through the *meaning* of the spoken word. One would not really read if he associated the written word only with alphabetic characters or parts of speech. This is useful only for explaining the *theory* of a language once reading ability has been developed. It is words—not letters or theory—which have meaning for reading comprehension. A child is first taught to read only those words which are part of his spoken vocabulary. By discovering new and unfamiliar words through generalization and abstraction, he continues to increase this reading vocabulary. During this process reading becomes a sequential independent activity that serves as a necessary tool for more comprehensive types of learning.

As a logical parallel, an oral vocabulary (the "speaking") of music is a necessary requisite for learning to read music. Singing and rhythmic movement represent the "speaking" of music. Understanding of music is acquired through aural perception of tonality, kinesthetic feeling for meter, and sensitivity to musical expression developed through singing and rhythmic activities. As suggested by DeYarman (10), Dittemore (11), Lowery (19), Mainwaring (20), and Nye (24), to be able to read music, one must *hear* and *feel*, as an outcome of rote performance, what one *sees* in music notation. One then transmits this understanding through the voice or through the medium of a musical instrument.

In accordance with his basic musical aptitudes for developing tonal sense and rhythmic feeling, a person acquires an oral vocabulary of tonal and rhythm patterns. The research of Bean (2), Broman (7), Mainwaring (21), Ortmann (26), Petzold (28), and Van Nuys and Weaver (42) implies that the development of an oral vocabulary (by rote) of significant tonal and rhythm patterns constitutes the *experience* through which meaning is given to music, so that musical meaning can be associated with music notation for reading comprehension (just as a rote vocabulary of phrases of the spoken word constitutes the vehicle through which meaning is given to the written word). Like the relationship of the alphabet to language, the spelling of pitch names and the fractional values of notes are useful only as *theoretical* explanations of music notation after one has already acquired the functional ability of reading music through meaning. Because it takes more than one note to make a meaningful tonal or rhythmic pattern, the knowledge of the pitch name or of the arithmetic value of one isolated note does not constitute readiness or ability to read music.

One may be said to have acquired basic music enjoyment and understanding when he has developed his tonal and rhythm imagery. This is demonstrated by the ability to respond aurally to tonal patterns and to feel rhythm patterns kinesthetically, as suggested by Dalcroze (9), as well as to interpret elements (including timbre and form) when listening to music. Further, basic musical enjoyment and understanding by their very nature provide the readiness for developing music literacy, the reading and writing of music. After an individual develops music literacy readiness (that is, a sense of tonality, rhythmic feeling, and musical expression) in accordance with his musical aptitudes, the sequential development of music literacy ability, as indicated by Jersild and Bienstock (15), becomes a natural consequence.

To recognize best how rhythmic enjoyment and understanding are developed and ultimately culminate in rhythmic literacy, it is necessary that we first establish an operational definition of rhythm.

DEFINITION OF RHYTHM

Rhythm is comprised of three basic elements. They are 1) tempo beats, 2) meter beats, and 3) melodic rhythm. In music these elements interact in a composite polyrhythmic manner and give rise to what is referred to as rhythm.

Tempo Beats

Of the three basic elements of rhythm, tempo beats are fundamental because they provide the foundation upon which all other elements of rhythm are superimposed. The tempo beat is easily recognized as generally being the walking, marching, or swaying beat. Notational examples of tempo beats are given below.

The temporal consistency of tempo beats is of utmost importance because precision of higher aspects of rhythm, specifically meter and melodic rhythm, is dependent on this stability. Unless tempo beats are equally spaced in time (except, of course, when tempo is purposefully altered for expressive purposes), meter and melodic rhythm are affected. For example, the duration of a whole note in four-quarter meter cannot be appropriately interpreted unless tempo beats have organizational consistency; and dotted eighth- and sixteenth-note patterns in duple meter take on the character of triplets as tempo beats become faster.

Furthermore, without consistency of tempo beats, syncopation could not exist. It is interesting to note that the research of Coppock (8), DeYarman (10), Dittemore (11), and Pond and Moorhead (31) objectively supports the subjective opinions of some musicologists which suggests that human beings organize tempo beats into pairs.

Meter Beats

Meter—in music, poetry, and speech—"moves" in two's and three's. Duple meter is derived by superimposing two equally spaced beats within the duration of a tempo beat. Triple meter is derived by superimposing three equally spaced beats within the duration of a tempo beat. Notational examples of duple and triple meter beats, respectively, are given below.

Meter beats are of more importance to rhythm than tempo beats because when tempo beats are subjectively organized into pairs, meter is felt either as a group of two beats (which gives rise to duple meter) or as a group of three beats (which gives rise to triple meter) within the duration of each tempo beat. Meter is a distinguishing characteristic of melodic rhythm because melodic rhythm must be based on either duple or triple meter; if meter changes, melodic rhythm is affected. For example, a melodic rhythm pattern comprised of a dotted eighth and sixteenth note in $\frac{2}{4}$ would essentially become a quarter note followed by an eighth note pattern if the meter were changed to triple. Appropriate meter must be felt in order to place correctly notes in melodic rhythm which do not coincide with tempo beats. As tempo beats are fundamental to meter, meter is fundamental to melodic rhythm. Without being superimposed on meter, melodic rhythm would be disorganized.

Melodic Rhythm

Melodic rhythm comprises rhythm patterns that correspond to the rhythm of the melody or to the rhythm of the text. As indicated, these patterns are superimposed on meter beats and tempo beats. However, melodic rhythm patterns can be coincidental with meter beats and tempo beats, and they also may include fractionations and elongations of meter beats and elongations of tempo beats.

With the possible exception of the more complex concepts of harmonic and contrapuntal rhythm and of extended musical form, melodic rhythm provides the most important rhythmic function in music. Meter beats and tempo beats are fundamental to melodic rhythm, and melodic rhythm is fundamental to the tonal aspects of music. Without rhythm, melody would be difficult to organize and therefore to perceive and conceptualize.

ORGANIZATION OF RHYTHM PATTERNS

As indicated, the three basic counterparts of rhythm—tempo beats, meter beats, and melodic rhythm—elicit musical meaning when the *relationship* between two or more notes (or rests) comprises a rhythmic pattern in the mind of the listener. Melodic rhythm cannot be thought of as only one note. Rhythm patterns exist as a result of the interaction among notes and rests. They generally include at least two notes and rests, and in practical usage they comprise up to six notes.

Because every melodic rhythm pattern is indigenous to a specific meter, patterns might be best classified according to metrical type: 1) Basic Duple, 2) Basic Triple, 3) Uncommon Duple, 4) Uncommon Triple, 5) Basic Mixed, 6) Uncommon Mixed, 7) Basic Unusual, and 8) Uncommon Unusual. The terms "basic" and "uncommon" refer to the frequency with which the patterns are found in music; the more numerous basic patterns are found more often in music. The terms "duple" and "triple," like those of "mixed" and "unusual," correspond to types of meter. Both duple and triple are considered usual meter in contrast to mixed and unusual meter.

From the examples below it can be seen that basic duple patterns include rests, syncopation, and upbeats (on the bottom line). In a strict sense, however, upbeats are not really independent patterns because they combine with, and necessarily become part of, the patterns they precede.

BASIC DUPLE PATTERNS

As with duple meter, the following examples of basic triple patterns include rests, syncopation, and upbeats (on the bottom line). However, although there are more basic triple patterns than duple, the first four on the upper line are most frequently used.

BASIC TRIPLE PATTERNS

Uncommon patterns, both duple and triple, include notes and rests of longer duration and also ties. It can be seen from the examples below that they also comprise syncopation and upbeats (on the bottom lines). However, in contrast to basic duple and triple syncopated patterns, uncommon duple and triple syncopated patterns are more complex. And, unlike basic duple and triple upbeat patterns, uncommon duple and triple upbeat patterns begin on a tempo beat.

UNCOMMON DUPLE PATTERNS

Only duple and triple *meter beats* constitute basic mixed patterns. These patterns are used in conjunction with a contrasting duple or

UNCOMMON TRIPLE PATTERNS

triple meter signature and they are notated as duplets $\frac{6}{8}$ ♩♩ or triplets

$\frac{2}{4}$ ♩♩♩ , respectively; this produces mixed meter. Uncommon mixed patterns are analogous to the remaining basic and uncommon duple and triple patterns but notated, of course, within duplet and triplet groupings. Patterns which incorporate a quintuplet, sextolet, or septuplet all belong in this category.

Unusual patterns differ from mixed patterns in two very important respects. First, in mixed meter (as in usual meter), tempo beats are consistent in time (spaced equally distant) but meter beats are inconsistent in time; duplets and triplets (as they function as meter beats) are temporally expanded and contracted, respectively, to conform to the pulse of the tempo beat. Conversely, in unusual meter, meter beats are not notated as duplets and triplets and therefore are consistent in time. As a result, tempo beats (except for some unusual patterns in $\frac{3}{4}$ and $\frac{9}{8}$, where meter beats are consistently grouped in either two's or in three's respectively) become inconsistent in time. Second, unusual patterns necessarily comprise a complete measure.

It can be seen from the following examples that there are four types of basic unusual patterns. On the top line are examples comprising just two tempo beats with meter beats grouped in two's and in three's; on the second line are examples comprising more than a pair of tempo beats including both duple and triple meter beats; on the third line are examples comprising more than two tempo beats with some tempo beats being void of meter; and on the bottom line are examples comprising just three tempo beats with meter beats consistently grouped in either two's or in three's. Uncommon unusual patterns include the other basic and uncommon duple and triple patterns which are superimposed on, and therefore performed with, temporarily consistent meter beats. Also, polyrhythmic patterns belong in this category.

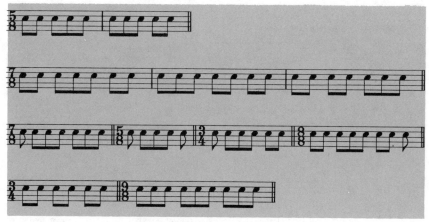

BASIC UNUSUAL PATTERNS

RHYTHM READINESS

The ability to feel rhythm patterns kinesthetically constitutes rhythm readiness. It provides the basis for the rhythmic interpretation of style in music, especially jazz and popular music (including folk music), and this eurhythmic activity also provides readiness for the development of rhythm literacy. The fundamental role of eurhythmics in acquiring rhythmic understanding is well pronounced in the research findings of Bond (4), Boyle (6), Heinlein (14), Mainwaring (20, 21), Seashore (34), Thackray (39), Williams (44), and Wright (45).

As described by Dalcroze (9), the initial stage of rhythm readiness is the development of large muscle creative and interpretive activity. After this type of bodily freedom is achieved, more complex types of rhythmic responses (such as simultaneous bodily movements involving smaller muscle activities) are developed. Through typical uninhibited (not rigid or tense) activities—such as marching, walking, swinging arms, running on tempo beats, and/or clapping or tapping meter beats—students develop an understanding of consistent tempo as they discriminate between duple and triple meter. Heinlein (14), indirectly suggests it is possible that during these readiness stages a feeling for consistency of tempo can be impaired if "tempo rubato" is introduced other than at phrase endings.

Spontaneous activities of young children, as observed by Pond and Moorhead (31), suggest that they react to triple meter, in pairs of tempo beats, before duple meter (this may be due in part to the fact that triple meter is a tense meter as compared to the more relaxed feeling associated with duple meter). However, music teachers have learned that children are able to perform both meters equally well as they physically react to rote songs and to recorded music. Older students further develop an understanding of tempo and meter by engaging in more sophisticated rhythm activities such as dancing, conducting, and performing on rhythm instruments and on the autoharp, ukulele, and guitar.

By associating eurhythmic feeling with rhythm syllable patterns Bolden (4), one of few researchers who have investigated the subject, found that students efficiently and practicably develop rhythm literacy readiness in the same 'manner as when the "number" or "Tonic Sol-fa" syllable pattern vocabulary is used for tonal literacy readiness. By not first having to memorize the value names of individual notes or the function of their fractional values in order to try to read rhythm notation, students are able to develop rhythm reading ability before they are formally taught the arithmetic function of fractions in the intermediate grades.

Because time value names of notes cannot be chanted effectively for reading rhythm patterns, some music educators have advocated action words, rather than syllables, to represent patterns. For example, "run-ning" is associated with eighth note patterns in $\frac{2}{4}$, "walk-ing" with quarter note patterns in $\frac{2}{4}$, and "gal-lop-ing" with eighth note patterns in $\frac{6}{8}$. The major limitation of this approach is that it is able to accommodate only a few basic rhythm patterns and no uncommon patterns. Mnemonic words are preferred by other music teachers; for example, "Mississippi" can be represented in notational form by four consecutive sixteenth notes in $\frac{2}{4}$ and "Amsterdam" by three consecutive eighth notes in $\frac{6}{8}$. Although habits of pronunciation are less consistent than physical reactions, the mnemonic and action word approaches would seem therefore to incorporate even more weaknesses. The "1 e and a" system, emphasized particularly by instrumental music teachers, encompasses the fewest limitations of all systems thus far described. Unfortunately, however, in this system, no strict provision is made for triple meter patterns.

From a logical analysis it can be concluded that to be most practicable, rhythm syllables should 1) be fundamentally different for patterns in duple, triple, and unusual meters, for tempo beats, and for each successive meter beat, 2) provide for all basic and uncommon patterns, 3) be easily articulated vocally, 4) not be associated with individual note values, and 5) not conflict in name with tonal syllables. Most importantly, a note (or rest) must be associated with a rhythm syllable by virtue of the positional (metrical) *relationship* of that note (or rest) to other notes in a given rhythm pattern and not solely according to its *fractional value name*.

Illustrated below are examples of syllables employed in more comprehensive rhythm pattern systems:

On the top line above the notation are the syllables used by Richards (32, 33), which were adapted from Kodály. It can be observed from an examination of the corresponding rhythm notation that the same syllables, as suggested by Richards, are used with both duple and triple meter patterns and for different meter beats, syllable names are associated with note fractional values, and that no syllable distinction is made between tempo and meter beat functions. Also, some of the syllables conflict in name with Tonic Sol-fa tonal syllables and cannot be easily articulated.

Examples of the French Time Name syllables (16) are given on the bottom line above the notation in the illustration. In this system fewer syllables are used with both duple and triple meter patterns, but otherwise, its limitations are similar to those of the adapted Kodály system. With musically sophisticated students, the French Time Name approach would probably prove to be superior because it makes provision for more complex patterns such as a sixteenth note triplet. In contrast to this system, Richards assigns to triplets syllables that are different from the syllables used in conjunction with three consecutive eighth notes in $\frac{6}{8}$.

The syllables below the notation in the illustration exemplify five important properties discussed previously. A further advantage of these syllables is that they are easily articulated with the tongue and therefore can be employed while one plays a wind instrument without necessarily impairing embouchure. The *ne* is pronounced like *na* in *nation,* na like *no* in *notch,* ni like *ne* in *neat,* and ta like *to* in *topic.* Although the same syllables are logically used regardless of whether a pattern appears in mixed or usual meter, different syllables (possibly 1 *be* or 1 *ba bi,* for groups of two's or three's, respectively) should be used with unusual meter patterns. But, as in duple and triple meter, the same syllable may be used for meter beat subdivisions in unusual patterns because it does not impinge on tempo beat or meter beat functions. Numbers, regardless of meter type, are always associated with tempo beats.

Regardless of the rhythm syllable system used, when learning rhythm syllables by rote (and when using them for reading purposes), it is suggested that the appropriate duple or triple *meter* syllables be performed or silently felt in order to place correctly all syllables in a rhythm pattern. This procedure also helps one feel rests precisely, because rhythm syllables corresponding to the notes for which rests are substituted can be silently "chanted." In a similar way, rhythm patterns comprising ties, notes, and rests of longer duration are best interpreted when meter beat syllables are felt as part of, and in association with, note and rest duration.

DeYarman's (10) and Dittemore's (11) findings, followed the logical implications of Bolden's (4) research, suggest that after students develop organized kinesthetic reaction to tempo and meter by performing a variety of duple and triple meter music (including songs comprising three and five measure phrases as well as those of two and four measures), rhythm syllables should first be associated only with duple and triple meter beat and tempo beat patterns. Children develop a vocabulary (by feeling, not sight) for these eight combined basic patterns, illustrated below, by singing songs, listening to recorded music, and performing rhythmic chants, echoes, rondos, dialogues, and rounds with and without rhythm instruments.

DeYarman (10) and Dittemore (11) further imply that after children learn these eight basic syllable patterns by rote, they are ready to develop a rote rhythm syllable vocabulary for the remaining basic and the uncommon duple and triple patterns. Then basic and uncommon mixed syllable patterns and finally basic and uncommon unusual patterns may be learned by rote.

Individual Differences in Rhythm Readiness

Although Groves (13), Klauer (17), Mainwaring (20), and Petzold (28) suggest that training has little or no effect on improving students' rhythmic achievement, other researchers have obtained more positive results. Pflederer (29) noted that in spite of the fact that older students learn more efficiently than younger students and that rhythmic understanding is more easily taught than tonal understanding, all students generally react favorably to instruction. Earlier Jersild and Bienstock (15) and Pond and Moorhead (31) also found that rhythmic training produced constructive results. Skornika (37) maintains that rhythmic instruction given at an early age is most beneficial in later effecting rhythm reading achievement in instrumental music. Moreover, the research results of Andrews and Diehl (1), Selzer (35), Sievers (36), and Vance and Grandprey (41) indicate that rhythmic achievement can be objectively evaluated at various levels of development. These findings indirectly suggest that instruction in rhythm is advantageous.

Probably the most relevant and instructive results pertaining to rhythmic training are found in studies which were designed to investigate individual differences among students. Drake (12) found his subjects to be quite variable in their ability to comprehend rhythmic tasks. Heinlein (14) reported that only two of eight students could adequately respond to tempo beats as they engaged in eurhythmic activities. And Linger (18) not only observed vast differences among students in their ability to perform rhythmically but also found considerable disagreement among students in their choice of an appropriate tempo for a given piece of music.

Obviously children develop rhythmic achievement in accordance with their rhythm aptitudes. It would seem, therefore, that instruction in general music and instrumental music classes would be most meaningful when it is adapted to the individual musical differences among students. The deficiencies of the less able students should be compensated for while the strengths of more gifted students are enhanced. As a result of this procedure, it is known that the differences in achievement among students become more extreme, but the overall achievement level of a class improves.

Individual musical needs, in regard to developing rhythm readiness, are most efficiently met within a *group situation*. For example, after a fundamental understanding of consistent tempo and duple and triple meter has been developed, students with lower aptitude are best able to continue to use large muscle activities as higher aptitude students engage in small muscle activities or in rhythm instrument performance, as both groups concurrently respond to music. Students with higher aptitude easily react to both tempo beats and meter beats as less able students react comfortably to either tempo beats or meter beats. Gifted students are sooner able to perform tempo beats, meter beats, and melodic rhythm simultaneously through clapping, tapping, and chanting.

In rhythmic echoes, dialogues, rondos, rounds, and chants, lower aptitude students are able to chant a simple meter syllable pattern while others perform on instruments or sing. With the echo technique specifically, simple patterns are easily performed by less competent students and relatively more complex patterns by more gifted students. Likewise, in the use of preplanned and creative dialogues and rondos, students can be expected to respond with musical answers which correspond to their aptitude. For example, a gifted student is able to respond with a triple meter pattern to a duple pattern, or two or more of these students are capable of performing a polyrhythmic pattern.

RHYTHM READING AND WRITING

After students have developed a *rote* vocabulary of the eight basic duple and triple rhythm syllable patterns, they are able to begin reading these patterns by associating what they feel with what they see in *traditional* notational form. Some music educators, such as Richards (33), indicate that students should first associate rhythm patterns only with note stems, beams, and dots. Nye (24) suggests/that lines of differential length serve well for introductory rhythm reading purposes, and Jones (16) reports a special type of rhythm notation sometimes used in conjunction with the French Tonic Sol-fa System, before students learn to read traditional rhythm notation. The research of Osborn (27), Peitersen (30), and Trismen (40) indicates that the benefits of reading spaced notation (where the distance between notes in a score is relative to the time value of the notes) do not transfer when traditional notation is encountered. The results of research bearing on the effectiveness of programmed instruction as an aid in efficiently developing rhythmic reading achievement have been positive. Mears (23) and Wardian (43) report such findings when traditional rhythmic notation is used.

Because there is no objective evidence to demonstrate that introductory systems for reading traditional rhythm notation are at all practicable, it would seem that until additional information is forthcoming, students might best begin to read basic patterns in traditional notational form. As students learn to read combinations of basic tempo beat and meter beat patterns, they are capable of learning concurrently the remaining basic and the uncommon duple and triple meter patterns and the basic and uncommon mixed and unusual meter patterns by *rote*. Then they may learn to read these more complex patterns in traditional notational form.

It is not reasonable to expect students to learn to read rhythm notation by chanting rhythm syllables or by naming rhythm syllables *from the beginning through the end of a song* (although they may profitably chant the melodic rhythm of a song with syllables as a *rote* activity). As previously indicated, we learn to read rhythm patterns in *phrases,* just as we read in phrases in our spoken language. Rhythm notation is more efficiently interpreted by silently associating rhythm *patterns* (phrases) in notational form with correlate *rhythm syllable patterns* learned by rote. In this way, songs can be sung using the *text* (not syllables) because students will learn to read melodic rhythm patterns sequentially and will rhythmically connect the patterns into phrases by internally feeling *meter* as they sing the words.

When *first* introduced to reading and writing rhythm notation, it would appear that students deal best with only one duple and one triple meter signature—for example, $\frac{2}{4}$ and $\frac{6}{8}$ or $\frac{4}{4}$ and $\frac{3}{4}$. The reason for this is that rhythm patterns which *sound the same* will, of course, *look different* in notational form when different sets of numbers are employed in *meter signatures.* To try *initially* to learn to read the same rhythm pattern written with different numbers in the lower part of a meter signature is analogous to trying to learn to read a passage in more than one language concurrently. Only after students can read in $\frac{2}{4}$ and $\frac{6}{8}$, for example (and after arithmetical fractions have been introduced by the classroom teacher), should they be exposed to the theory of rhythm notation and learn how to read music which utilizes meter signatures with different numerical combinations.

Once students begin to read music notation, they can easily learn to write rhythm patterns. It is important that students learn to notate rhythm, not only as a means of furthering their appreciation of music, but also for the continued expansion and development of their reading ability. Educational psychologists are aware that students who can write, read better than those who cannot write. Students may best learn writing skill by notating chants dictated with rhythm or neutral syllables, performed on rhythm instruments, or heard on a recording. Students should be able to write from memory patterns based on familiar music and also notate responses to rhythm echoes, rondos, chants, dialogues, and rounds. Rhythm instrument accompaniments may also be notated.

Music literacy, like English literacy, is developed in cyclical fashion. Students over and over again see the same relatively few important patterns as they perform music. Every time a pattern is encountered, it takes on new meaning which, in turn, prepares students for further understanding. Students learn by means of transference and generalization to read and write rhythm patterns not necessarily taught to them by rote. Although research (10) and (11) suggests that students should first learn to read and write rhythm patterns which comprise combinations of only tempo beats and meter beats, there is no hierarchy for learning additional rhythm patterns. Generally, patterns which students are currently learning to read and write should be derived from literature that they are performing, and, for review purposes, from literature with which they are familiar.

That there are various ways of writing the same rhythm pattern (depending upon the meter signature) may initially seem odd to students. However, as in all symbolic languages, notation has developed over a period of time and inconsistencies have occurred. (Consider George Bernard Shaw's description of inconsistency in English spelling: the word *fish* could be interpreted and read as the word *ghoti* since the *gh* has an *f* sound as in the word *enough*, the *o* an *i* sound as in the word *women*, and the *ti* an *sh* sound as in the word *nation*.) Students probably learn to compensate for inconsistencies in the English language because of the quality and quantity of their training in speaking and reading that language. Given an acceptable foundation in rhythm readiness, they should be expected to compensate similarly for inconsistencies in musical notation.

In summary, it must be emphasized that students are often erroneously taught to memorize the time value names of notes for the purpose of learning how to read and write rhythm. As previously indicated, when fractional value names of notes (such as whole, half, quarter, eighth, etc.) are learned as isolated facts, they have only negligible worth for learning to read rhythm notation *musically*. Simply knowing the fractional value of isolated notes does not necessarily contribute to the kinesthetic interpretation of a *rhythm pattern* seen in notational form. This knowledge basically helps one to understand the grammar of rhythm notation after he can read and write rhythm.

Individual Differences in Rhythm Reading and Writing

As research has suggested in the case of readiness skills, when students are taught rhythm literacy skills, individual differences in their rhythm aptitudes should be considered. For example, as less able students continue to perform echo, rondo, and dialogue responses, more able students might be directed to notate those responses or to read specific dialogue responses. Gifted students can be expected to write patterns from memory, whereas less gifted students need to see and hear again and again what they are to write. More able students easily learn to notate patterns representing their creative (or improvised) dialogue responses. These students find it challenging to write in duple meter a pattern the class is learning to read in triple meter and vice versa.

Generally, rhythm literacy skills of less able students can be improved if they rewrite rhythm patterns in longhand notation (converting a dotted note to two or more tied notes, or a three-note syncopated pattern to a pattern of four or more notes of which two or more notes are tied, for example). More able students may rewrite the pattern with appropriate "substitute" symbols, such as incorporated rests.

THEORY OF RHYTHM NOTATION

After students have learned to read and write rhythm using only one duple and one triple meter signature (and after they begin the arithmetic study of fractions) it seems reasonable to assume that they are then ready to read and write rhythm patterns in other meter signatures. A logical manner in which students can learn the interpretation of additional meter signatures is presented in the following section.

The meaning of a meter signature is generally thought of in a limiting way. The traditional, but erroneous, definition of a meter signature (more commonly referred to as a time signature), such as $\frac{2}{4}$, is "two beats (or counts) in a measure and a quarter note gets one beat (or count)." More fully and correctly, $\frac{2}{4}$ indicates that the music will move in duple meter and a quarter note will represent a *tempo* beat; $\frac{6}{8}$ indicates that the music will move in triple meter and an eighth note will represent a *meter* beat. From the latter interpretation, the musical function of rhythm imagery is activated kinesthetically. When the traditional definition is used, one is confronted merely with solving an arithmetic problem.

When a student *first* reads rhythm notation (using only one duple and one triple meter signature) with rhythm syllables (and *necessarily* without a formal understanding of note fraction values), all he needs to understand is that the upper number of a meter signature indicates the meter of the music. The meaning of a lower number need not be considered until the theory of rhythm notation, specifically note values, is introduced as an aid in reading music that comprises unfamiliar meter signatures. This suggests that it is relatively unimportant to think of the meter signature itself as having an arithmetic function. The lower number of a meter signature is only an explanation of the specific *arbitrary* manner in which the melodic rhythm has been written as it arithmetically relates to tempo beats and meter beats. As a matter of fact, for initial reading, $\frac{2}{4}$ could be written as $\frac{2}{A}$, $\frac{2}{B}$, or $\frac{2}{Z}$ and $\frac{6}{8}$ as $\frac{6}{A}$, $\frac{6}{B}$, or $\frac{6}{Z}$ without sacrificing any functional understanding on the part of students.

When a student begins to read and write in more than two meter signatures, he learns that the upper numbers 2 and 4 of a meter signature indicate the music will move in duple meter and that the upper numbers 3, 6, and 12 indicate the music will move in triple meter. The upper number 2 indicates that the music will be *written* as based on two groups of duple meter beats in a measure. The upper number 4 indicates that the music will be *written* as based on four groups of duple meter beats in a measure. Similarly, the upper numbers 3, 6, and 12 indicate that the music will be *written* as based on one, two, and four groups of triple meter beats in a measure, respectively. Even though music may be written with a $\frac{4}{4}$ meter signature, children do not *feel* tempo beats as "1, 2, 3, 4," but rather, "1, 2, 1, 2," as if each measure were actually written like two measures of $\frac{2}{4}$ or one measure of $\frac{2}{2}$ (¢), depending on the dictates of the music. Likewise, when reading music with a $\frac{12}{8}$ meter signature, students do not *feel* tempo beats as "1, 2, 3, 4," but rather, "1, 2, 1, 2," as if every measure were written like two measures of $\frac{6}{8}$. For music written with a $\frac{3}{4}$ meter signature, children generally *feel* "1, 2," as if every two measures were written like one measure of $\frac{6}{8}$ (or $\frac{6}{4}$)—that is, children usually *feel* $\frac{3}{4}$ as *one* tempo beat comprising triple meter regardless of speed of tempo beats. However, on rare occasions, when students *feel* $\frac{3}{4}$ (or $\frac{6}{8}$) as three tempo beats comprising duple meter, the phrasing has undoubtedly given rise to a specific type of unusual meter as previously described.

As indicated, the rhythm of music is not always *written* the way it is *felt*. Regardless of notational practice, young children usually subjectively organize tempo beats in pairs such as "1 –2" (or as "1 –1, 2" or "1, 2 –1," as found in unusual meter). Therefore, written music with one or four tempo beats to a measure, for example, appears to be an artifact. Just why music is written with a 12 or 4 as an upper number of a meter signature is debatable. It may be that composers think different upper numbers result in different types of phrasing. However, rhythm based on a 12 (or 3) or 4 in the upper number of a meter signature could just as well be based on a 6 or 2, respectively; and phrase lines, tempo, dynamics, and rhythm markings could be employed for objective phrasing instructions. Of course, there is always the simple supposition that the upper number 12 or 4 is used to reduce the number of measure lines required for writing music although the upper number 3 necessitates the use of more measure lines.

Students easily generalize the *meaning* of $\frac{4}{4}$ from $\frac{2}{4}$, or vice versa, because the lower number in both meter signatures is the same and therefore the rhythm patterns are written alike. Similarly, the interpretation of patterns written in $\frac{6}{4}$ and then $\frac{3}{4}$ are generalized (*through the use of syllables*) from corresponding patterns written in $\frac{6}{8}$ with which students are familiar. Students best learn to read and write in new meter signatures when they do not have to cope with learning the function of *two* different numbers, upper and lower, simultaneously.

As stated, the lower number of a meter signature simply describes the kind of note associated with a tempo beat or a meter beat. Once the lower number of a meter signature is related to a specific note and rest name and its correlate fractional value, the *theory* of melodic rhythm is easily comprehended. That is, if a quarter note represents the tempo beat, then two eighth notes will constitute a duple meter pattern; again, if a quarter note represents the tempo beat, then the melodic rhythm of the tempo beat subdivided into four equal parts is written with four sixteenth notes. Editors of some music anthologies have developed a practical notational scheme for meter signatures. Instead of writing a lower number in a meter signature, ($\frac{2}{4}$) for example, there appears the

actual note that the number represents ($\frac{2}{\rho}$).

From the foregoing discussion, it should be apparent that a meter signature is *not a fraction* and should not be interpreted or written as a fraction; that is, with a line between the two numbers like $\frac{2}{4}$. (If a student is taught that a meter signature is a fraction, his natural inclination would be to reduce $\frac{2}{4}$ to $\frac{1}{2}$). The only justification for considering a meter signature as a fraction would be that, for example, a measure of $\frac{2}{4}$ would contain the equivalent of one half a whole note. However, this emphasis on a whole note is not educationally sound because, for meter signatures other than $\frac{4}{4}$, a complete measure is not equal in fractional time to a whole note. In addition, the possession of this arithmetical knowledge in no way promotes kinesthetic rhythmic feeling which is so necessary for the *musical* interpretation of a meter signature. It would be well to refer verbally to the meter signature $\frac{2}{4}$, for example, as two-*quarter* and not two-*four*. Likewise, $\frac{2}{8}$ should be called two-*eighth* and not two-*eight*, $\frac{2}{2}$ should be two-*half* and not two-*two*, etc. The correct verbal definition of a meter signature refers to the lower number as a note value, which in fact it is. The incorrect definition forces extra and unnecessary thought on the part of the student because he has to transform, for example, a *two* to a *half*, in order to understand what kind of a note, in fact, represents a tempo beat or meter beat.

A related problem specifically associated with defining, for example, the meter signature $\frac{6}{8}$ as "six beats in a measure and an eighth note gets one beat," or $\frac{3}{4}$ as "three beats in a measure and a quarter note gets one beat" is that the definition is incomplete and therefore technically unsound. The meter signature $\frac{6}{8}$ generally indicates that the rhythm of the music will move in triple (usual) meter and will be written as based on two groups of triple meter beats in a measure. Consistent with this is the fact that a dotted quarter note and *not* an eighth note will "get" a (*tempo*) beat. An eighth note in this meter will represent one *meter* beat. The reason that the meaning of the $\frac{6}{8}$ and the $\frac{3}{4}$ meter signature is commonly misinterpreted is because with traditional symbols it is not possible to indicate that a dotted quarter note or a dotted half note represents a tempo beat. In other words, there is no number that can be used in the lower part of a meter signature that would represent a dotted note value. Instead of indicating two beats of a triple as $\overset{2}{\flat}\cdot$ for example, the meter signature $\frac{6}{8}$ has been traditionally employed; and instead of indicating one beat of the triple as $\overset{1}{\flat}\cdot$, $\frac{3}{4}$ is conveniently substituted. As an unfortunate result, the method for interpreting duple meter signatures (in which the upper and lower numbers refer to *tempo* beats) has been incorrectly generalized to the interpretation of triple meter signatures (in which the upper and lower numbers refer to *meter* beats). The following, then, must be understood for correctly interpreting the meaning of meter signatures: both numbers of a duple signature refer to the tempo beat ($\frac{2}{4}$ means that the music will be written as based on *two tempo* beats (2) in a measure and a quarter note (4) will represent a *tempo* beat); both numbers of a triple signature refer to the meter beat ($\frac{6}{8}$ means that the music will be written as based on *six meter* beats (6) in a measure and an eighth note (8) will represent a *meter* beat); and both numbers in an unusual meter signature (except when $\frac{3}{4}$ is used) refer to the meter beat ($\frac{5}{8}$ means that the music will be written as based on *five meter* beats (5) in a measure, and an eighth note (8) will represent a *meter* beat). Most often the meter signature $\frac{6}{8}$ indicates *two beats of triple* and not *three beats of duple* and $\frac{3}{4}$, *one beat of triple* and not *three beats of duple*. If in fact a composer meant to imply three beats of duple and not one or two beats of triple for $\frac{3}{4}$ and $\frac{6}{8}$, respectively, he would indicate this in an appropriate manner, and the experienced musician would correctly perform the music in unusual meter.

For the purpose of learning the value of notes and the *complete* meaning of a meter signature, traditional charts that emphasize memoriter types of instructional procedures are insufficient. Students can learn these facts in a more practical, functional, and interesting manner within a musical context. As indicated in the discussion about teaching to the individual needs of musically gifted students, older students easily learn to read and write a familiar duple meter pattern using a different duple signature, or to "transpose" a duple meter pattern to triple meter or vice versa. They are also able to notate a rhythm pattern chanted or performed on a rhythm instrument with an uncommon meter signature such as $\frac{6}{16}$ or $\frac{3}{16}$. Rhythm echo, rondo, and dialogue responses are also appropriately used in this connection. Suffice it to say that it is more beneficial for students to learn the theory of rhythm notation by working with the feeling of rhythm than by being told to memorize the isolated and nonfunctional arithmetic definition that "two half notes equal a whole note," etc.

Finally, from ancillary research, a few points merit emphasis: 1) Students can learn to read and write rhythm much easier when beamed notation is used. Typical vocal notation, represented by separated (flagged) notes, makes it difficult to visually identify rhythm patterns and comprehend rhythmic relationships among notes. Consider the ease in reading a rhythm pattern consisting of three barred eighth notes with a $\frac{6}{8}$ meter signature, for example, as compared to reading this same pattern with three flagged notes, especially if note stems go in different directions. 2) Particularly when instrumentalists "sightread" music, they are basically reading rhythm (that is, note stems and beams) and to a lesser extent tonal elements. 3) Rhythm notation is often written in "shorthand" with an eighth note–quarter note–eighth note, for example, rather than the "longhand" notation of four eighth notes with the second and third notes tied. Students can learn to read rhythm patterns written in "shorthand" (in association with unfamiliar meter signatures) with greater ease once they understand correlate "longhand" notation; ties are used to facilitate the interpretation of syncopated patterns and other patterns which include dotted notes, half notes, and longer notes. 4) When dealing with note "values" in a dotted quarter note and eighth pattern in $\frac{2}{4}$ for example, students find it difficult to comprehend that the former "gets a beat and a half" because they generally think of "1" as a tempo beat and the half as just the second half of that tempo beat. (When counting rhythm, we say "1" as we begin the first beat but we do not "have" one beat until we begin "2.") It is more efficient to interpret the *duration* of a dotted quarter note in $\frac{2}{4}$ as one tempo beat plus the next meter beat or as the equivalent of three meter beats. 5) There are no so-called *melodic rhythm* accents defined according to the placement of a bar (measure) line. Supposedly, the original function of a bar line was only to guide the visual process in reading complex notation. In actual practice, accents are provided by the pulse of the underlying meter upon which the notes of a melodic rhythm pattern are based (regardless of their position in the measure) in accordance with appropriate rhythm markings and judicious musical interpretation. 6) Rhythm notation is not exact and therefore only *suggests* the interaction of rhythmic accent and note duration that a composer intended. The interpretation of rhythm, as dictated by musical style and personal taste, may render identically notated patterns differently.

SUMMARY

Rhythm is comprised of three basic elements. They are 1) tempo beats, 2) meter beats, and 3) melodic rhythm. In music, these counterparts interact in a composite "polyrhythmic" manner and give rise to what is generally referred to as rhythm.

Students develop perceptual rhythmic understanding primarily by engaging in eurhythmic activities. After they are able to perceive and discriminate tempo beats, meter beats, and melodic rhythm, they have the readiness to develop rhythmic concepts that ultimately lead to rhythmic literacy. The ability to read and write rhythm is dependent on the degree to which a student can kinesthetically feel what he sees in notational form.

The three basic counterparts of rhythm elicit musical meaning when the *relationship* between two or more notes (or rests) comprises a rhythm pattern in the mind of the listener. Every melodic rhythm pattern is indigenous to either duple, triple, mixed, or unusual meter. Students may best conceptualize melodic rhythm patterns through the use of rhythm syllables.

For instruction in rhythm to be beneficial, the individual musical differences among students must be taken into account in the learning process. The deficiencies of less able students should be compensated for while the strengths of more gifted students are enhanced. It is well to remember that just as a person can never become completely mature, he cannot acquire perfect rhythmic achievement. He can only progressively aspire to such attainment.

STUDY GUIDE

1. Explain how perceptual learning relates to the study of rhythm.
2. Explain how conceptual learning relates to the study of rhythm.
3. Explain what is meant by rhythm readiness.
4. Explain what is meant by rhythm literacy.
5. Explain how rhythm readiness forms the basis for rhythm literacy.
6. Why is rhythm literacy so important to music understanding?
7. Why do isolated notes have no functional rhythmic value?
8. Explain the logic of why rhythm is best organized through patterns.
9. What qualities make rhythm syllables of practicable value?
10. Develop a definition of rhythm which would be understandable to elementary school children.
11. Develop a definition of a meter signature which would be understandable to elementary school children.
12. Why should students be introduced to only one duple and one triple meter signature when they first begin to read rhythm notation?

13. Explain the difference between the meter signature $\frac{2}{4}$ and $\frac{4}{4}$, and between $\frac{6}{8}$ and $\frac{12}{8}$.

14. Try to locate a piece of music written with the meter signature $\frac{4}{4}$ that does not sound like it is written in $\frac{2}{4}$ or cut time.

15. Develop and explain some techniques you would employ for teaching to the individual musical differences among students as they are studying rhythm.

BIBLIOGRAPHY

1. Andrews, Frances, and Ned Diehl, *Development of a Technique for Identifying Elementary School Children's Musical Concepts*. University Park: The Pennsylvania State University, 1967.

2. Bean, Kenneth L., "An Experimental Approach to the Reading of Music," *Psychological Monographs*, L (1938), 80.

3. Bean, Kenneth L., "Reading Music Instead of Spelling It," *The Journal of Musicology*, I (1939), 1–5.

4. Bolden, Joyce and Inez Johnson, "The Influence of Selected Factors on Growth in Sight Singing and Rhythmic Reading." Unpublished Ph.D. dissertation, Michigan State University, 1967.

5. Bond, M., "Rhythmic Perception and Gross Motor Performance," *Research Quarterly*, XXX (1959), 259–65.

6. Boyle, John David, "The Effects of Prescribed Rhythmical Movements on the Ability to Sight Read Music." Unpublished Ph.D. dissertation, University of Kansas, 1968.

7. Broman, Keith LaVern, "The Effects of Subjective Rhythmic Grouping Under the Influence of Variable Rates." Unpublished Ph.D. dissertation, University of Indiana, 1956.

8. Coppock, Doris E., *Development of an Objective Measure of Rhythmic Motor Response*. Unpublished Ph.D. dissertation, University of Iowa, 1964.

9. Dalcroze, Émil Jacques, *Rhythm, Music, and Education*. New York: G. P. Putnam's Sons, 1921.

10. DeYarman, Robert. "An Experimental Analysis of the Development of Rhythmic and Tonal Capabilities of Kindergarten and First Grade Children." Unpublished Ph.D. dissertation, University of Iowa, 1971.

11. Dittemore, Edgar, "An Investigation of Some Musical Capabilities of Elementary School Children." *Studies in the Psychology of Music*, VI (1970), 1–44.

12. Drake, Alan H., "An Experimental Study of Selected Variables in the Performance of Musical Duration Notation," *Journal of Research in Music Education*, XVI (1968), 329–38.

13. Groves, William C., "Rhythmic Training and Its Relationship to the Synchronization of Motor-Rhythmic Responses," *Journal of Research in Music Education*, XVII (1969), 408–15.

14. Heinlein, Christian Paul, "A New Method of Studying the Rhythmic Responses of Children Together with an Evaluation of the Method of Simple Observation," *Journal of Genetic Psychology*, XXXVI (1929), 205–28.

15. Jersild, Arthur, and Sylvia Bienstock, "Development of Rhythm in Young Children," Teachers College, Columbia University: *Child Development Monographs*, XXII (1935), 1–97.

16. Jones, Archie, *Music Education in Action*. Boston: Allyn & Bacon, 1960.

17. Klauer, Naomi, "The Effect of Training and Rhythm on Rhythm Discrimination in the Intermediate Grades." Unpublished Master's thesis, University of Iowa, 1924.

18. Linger, Bernard Lee, "An Experimental Study of Durational Notation." Unpublished Ph.D. dissertation, Florida State University, 1966.

19. Lowery, H., "On Reading Music," *Dioptical Review and British Journal of Physiological Optics*, I (1940), 78–88.

20. Mainwaring, James, "Experiments in the Analysis of Cognitive Processes Involved in Musical Ability and in Music Education," *British Journal of Educational Psychology*, I (1931), 180–203.

21. Mainwaring, James, "Kinesthetic Factors in the Recall of Musical Experience," *British Journal of Psychology*, XXIII (1933), 284–307.

22. Mainwaring, James, "The Assessment of Musical Ability," *British Journal of Educational Psychology*, XVII (1947), 83–96.

23. Mears, Wilfred G., "Tri-Sensory Reinforcement of a Rhythm Learning Program." Unpublished Ph.D. dissertation, Florida State University, 1965.

24. Nye, Robert, *Music for Elementary School Children*. Washington: The Center for Applied Research in Education, 1963.

25. Ohmann, Richard, "Grammar and Meaning," *The American Heritage Dictionary of the English Language*. Boston: Houghton Mifflin Company, 1969.

26. Ortmann, Otto, "Span of Vision in Note Reading," *Yearbook of the Music Educators National Conference* (1937), 88–93.

27. Osborn, Leslie A., "Notation Should Be Metric and Representational," *Journal of Research in Music Education*, XIV (1966), 67–83.

28. Peitersen, D. M., "An Experimental Evaluation of the Training Effects of Rhythm Training in Spaced Notation on Subsequent Reading of Commercially Printed Music." Unpublished Ph.D. dissertation, University of Minnesota, 1954.

29. Petzold, Robert, *Auditory Perception of Musical Sounds by Children in the First Six Grades.* Madison: University of Wisconsin Press, 1966.

30. Pflederer, Marilyn, "The Responses of Children to Musical Tasks Embodying Piaget's Principle of Conservation," *Journal of Research in Music Education,* XII (1964), 251–68.

31. Pond, Donald, and Gladys Moorhead, *Music of Young Children:* Part I, *Chant* (1941); Part II, *General Observations* (1942); Part III, *Free Use of Instruments for Musical Growth* (1943); Part IV, *Musical Notation* (1944). Santa Barbara: Pillsbury Foundation for the Advancement of Music Education.

32. Richards, Mary Helen, *The Fourth Year.* Palo Alto: Fearon Publishers, 1966.

33. Richards, Mary Helen, *Threshold to Music,* Palo Alto: Fearon Publishers, 1964.

34. Seashore, Robert, "Studies In Motor Rhythm," University of Iowa *Studies in Child Welfare,* II (1926), 149–99.

35. Selzer, Serkphine, "A Measure of the Singing and Rhythmic Development of Preschool Children," *Journal of Educational Psychology,* XXVII (1936), 417–24.

36. Sievers, C. H., "A Study of Rhythmic Performance with Social Consideration of the Factors Involved in the Formation of a Scale for Measuring Ability." Unpublished Ph.D. dissertation, University of Iowa, 1931.

37. Skornika, Joseph D., "The Function of Time and Rhythm in Instrumental Music Reading Competency." Unpublished D.Ed. dissertation, Oregon State University, 1958.

38. Smith, O. W., "Relationship of Rhythm Discrimination to Meter Rhythm Performance," *Journal of Applied Psychology,* XLI (1957), 365–69.

39. Thackray, Rupert, "Rhythmic Abilities and Their Measurement," *Journal of Research in Music Education,* XVII (1969), 144–48.

40. Trismen, Donald Albert, "An Experimental Investigation of a Maximal Speed Pacing Technique for Teaching Music Reading." Unpublished Ph.D. dissertation, Cornell University, 1964.

41. Vance, Franklyn, and Medora Grandprey, "Objective Methods of Ranking Nursery School Children on Certain Aspects of Musical Capacity," *Journal of Educational Psychology,* XXII (1931), 577–85.

42. Van Nuys, K., and H. E. Weaver, "Memory Span and Visual Pauses in Reading Rhythms and Melodies," *Psychological Monograph,* LV (1943), 33–50.

43. Wardian, Jeanne Foster, "An Experiment Concerning the Effectiveness of Programmed Learning for Use in Teaching the Fundamentals of Music." Unpublished D.Ed. dissertation, Washington State University, 1963.

44. Williams, H. M., "A Study in the Prediction of Motor Rhythmic Performance of School Children," *Journal of Genetic Psychology,* XLIII (1933), 377–88.

45. Wright, M., "The Effect of Training on Rhythm Ability and Other Problems Related to Rhythm," *Child Development,* VIII (1937), 159–72.

CHAPTER SIX

tonal learning

As stressed in the previous chapter, to read rhythm appropriately, one must *feel* what is seen in notational form. However, to read tones appropriately, one must *hear* what is seen in notational form. The ability to aurally perceive tonal patterns through musical imagery constitutes tonal reading readiness. Moreover, to be able to hear tonal relationships within and between patterns of tones represents evidence of one's ability to conceptualize musical sound, which is basic to musical enjoyment and understanding. Merely spelling and memorizing names of lines and spaces of the music staff and of key signatures do not necessarily enable one to hear what is seen in notational form, nor can it be realistically defended that such knowledge promotes musical enjoyment and understanding.

The importance of aural perception of tonal patterns through musical imagery for the purpose of developing musical understanding has been well established in the research literature. Agnew (1) found that accomplished musicians possess musical imagery on a greater and more refined scale than psychologists. Later, in theoretical analyses, Lowrey (43) and Mainwaring (45) deduced that aural perception provides the basis for organizing musical sound in a meaningful way. Bergan

(8) and Burroughs and Morris (12) corroborated the findings of Lowrey and Mainwaring through experimental research. Fowler (20) and Hewson (29) recently applied these psychological implications successfully in their development of methodological approaches to the teaching of musical understanding in the classroom.

There appears to be little doubt that musical sound is given meaning through a sense of tonality—that is, the musical mind aurally perceives sound and then conceptually organizes that sound into tonal meaning according to implications of the tonality (the resting tone and mode, and not necessarily the key) of the music. This operation is similar to the process of kinesthetically perceiving sound and then conceptually organizing rhythmic meaning of that sound through implied meter.

The early studies of Drexler (17) and Williams (72) demonstrated that a sense of tonality is fundamental to singing in tune and to remembering tunes. Even before the findings of these two researchers were available, Gordon (22) deduced the importance of a sense of tonality by demonstrating that children could recall a series of pitches based on a tonal center but not a series that did not imply a recognizable tonality. Blyler (9) and Bridges (11), working with young children, and Ritchie (60), who experimented with older students, found that children are partial to songs which easily lend themselves to tonal analysis and that melodic fragments based on diatonic harmony were more efficiently discriminated by students. The theoretical writings of Edwards (18) and Wunderlich (73, 74) are consistent with this research data, and the experimental results of DeYarman's (15) and Dittemore's (16) investigations of the role of a sense of tonality in cyclical musical learning patently indicate that students' progressive understanding of music is contingent on their developmental perception and conceptualization of tonal stress and stasis.

The results of the research bearing on tonal aspects of music practically suggest that, in correspondence with information theory, tones which comprise a melody are either relatively active or passive—that is, in a given key, some tones sound more "restful" and some tones sound more "restless" than others. Only one tone sounds most restful and that tone is called the resting tone, the tonal center, or the tonic. A sense of tonality is established when tonal relationships suggest one note (which may not even be comprised in the pattern) as being most restful; and from that objective resting tone, it can be established whether the music is in major or minor, or in less familiar modal tonality. As DeYarman (15), Dittemore (16), and Sherman (62) suggest, if the resting tone is not objective but a matter of subjective opinion, the pattern is considered by the intelligent listener to be nontonal—that is, it would lack traditional tonality to the trained ear.

Although a developed sense of tonality is basic for interpreting harmonic and contrapuntal functions, more pertinently, the establishment of a sense of tonality represents the readiness for melodic reading. However, it should be remembered that tonal achievement is very much dependent on tonal aptitude. Because a sense of tonality is efficiently developed through singing regardless of level of aptitude, a discussion of singing ranges and tessituras and of singing voices will be presented before an overall analysis of how students develop tonal understandings consistent with their level of tonal aptitude.

SINGING RANGES, TESSITURAS, AND VOICE BREAKS

The comparatively early studies of Jersild and Bienstock (33) and Hattwick (26) indicate that the songs in children's anthologies are too extreme in range. They consistently err by being too high, although bottom pitches at times are lower than need be. Kirkpatrick, nearly thirty years later, came to the same conclusion. From an analysis of the research data, it can be inferred that when students assume proper posture, appropriately use the diaphragm for substantial breath support, and sing songs that have an adequate tessitura (the range which comprises the *majority* of notes) and acceptable ranges, they develop good singing habits. Song ranges and tessituras that are extreme contribute to the development of nonsingers, and tessituras which continually cross voice breaks encourage students to sing out of tune. After the initial singing range (D above middle C to A, a perfect fifth above) is developed and sustained, it is naturally extended down to middle C to D, a major ninth above, for younger students, then down to A below middle C to E, a major twelfth above, for older students. The most comfortable tessitura for students of all ages (after the initial singing range is developed) extends from D, a major second above middle C, to B, a major sixth above. Ranges, tessituras, and voice breaks are illustrated below.

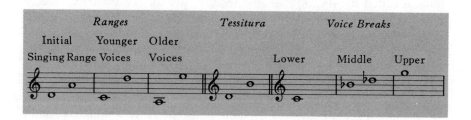

DEVELOPMENT OF SINGING VOICES

As Gould (23) and Smith (66) indicate, the term "monotone," which is used to characterize a nonsinger, has precarious implications. First, it suggests that a person is a nonsinger because of innate reasons, and second, it implies that he can produce only one "pitch." Neither implication has any basis in fact. Although Boardman (10) found that skills-oriented training did not improve vocal accuracy in preschool children, Gould (23), Jersild and Bienstock (34), and Smith (66) suggest that more appropriate types of training should prove to be beneficial.

It appears that, barring physical disability, anyone can learn to sing, just as anyone can learn to talk. (The degree to which *good tonal* habits are developed, however, is dependent upon tonal aptitude, just as what is said, after one learns to talk, is dependent upon intelligence. The term "monotone" is a nondescriptive term in that it implies only that a person is not a good singer. Actually there are various types of poor singers, and each requires unique help. There are nonsingers who try to sing in a speaking voice range, nonsingers who try to sing above the normal singing range, out-of-tune singers who lack a sense of melodic direction, out-of-tune singers who enjoy a sense of melodic direction but lack a sense of pitch, and an apparent "combination" type of nonsinger and out-of-tune singer. There are also singers who can sing with a group but not individually and singers who can sing individually but not well with a group.

Nonsingers

Not considering deafness or other physical disabilities as a factor, a nonsinger who tries to sing in a speaking voice range can learn to sing in a singing voice range. With children especially, a "singing voice" is not characterized by quality, but rather by voice placement in the continuum of pitch range. Children of kindergarten age and older speak in the range of approximately A below middle C up to middle C. The typical nonsinger is classified as a nonsinger because he tries to sing in this speaking voice range.

To learn to sing in a range appropriate for singing, such a person must become familiar, through "feeling" and "sound," with the throat muscles used for singing. The most efficient way to accomplish this is to yell. Through this procedure, a familiarity with the feeling of the muscles needed for singing becomes apparent. The yell is begun with an aspirate (h sound) for proper production: "Yoo-hoo"—sung "Hue-hoo"—creates good breath support. Echo yells, for aiding a nonsinger to produce sound in a singing voice, are confined to the initial singing range (D above middle C, to A, a perfect fifth above). A yell higher than this goes through or above the middle voice break (from approximately third line B♭ to D♭, a minor third above) and thereby constricts the throat muscles; to yell lower than this forces the voice below the lower voice break into the speaking voice range. Once a familiarity with the production of the yell is developed, the student is able to learn to soften and prolong the yell. This may be accomplished by pressing his palms tightly over his ears (this will make his voice sound more resonant to him) as he sings an echo response. Initially, after the nonsinger develops a singing voice, he will react like an out-of-tune singer who lacks a sense of melodic direction.

The student who tries to sing in a high tessitura, above the upper voice break (G a twelfth above middle C), is essentially also a nonsinger. His voice will lower into the proper singing voice range when he learns to sing *louder* through correct breathing habits. After the concept of diaphragmatic breath support is realized, the student will probably react like an out-of-tune singer who lacks a sense of pitch but not necessarily a sense of melodic direction. Echoes for this type of poor singer should emphasize the upper part of the initial singing range so that the student will not try to sing an octave higher.

Out-of-Tune Singers

It seems reasonable to assume that singers who sing out of tune have not developed a concept of tonality, and therefore they lack a sense of melodic direction or pitch, or both. An out-of-tune singer who lacks a sense of melodic direction is best seated near, or surrounded by, good singers because students learn to sing in tune more quickly by listening to their peers. Further, in order to learn to sing in tune, a student must often sing *individually*. This is easily accomplished in a *group* situation through the use of echo songs. If out-of-tune singers continually sing only with a group, they will use the class as a "crutch" and will not necessarily accept the responsibility of concentrating (listening), which is so necessary for the development of a sense of tonality. Simple major and harmonic minor echoes, consisting of three to five notes which *do not* move consecutively in the same melodic direction but necessarily comprise larger intervals, as suggested by Ortmann (51), are most suitable for out-of-tune singers. The initial singing range is best for these echo responses. After the student can sing in tune in this relatively limited singing range, his singing range will increase (from middle C, to D, a major ninth above). Initially however, the student cannot adequately sing echoes which *ascend diatonically* through the middle voice break but only those which *descend diatonically* through that voice break. That is, echoes should be sung which incorporate various ascending *interval skips* through the middle voice break (from second space A, or below, to D, a perfect fourth above), but *descending diatonic* movement through the middle voice break is acceptable. After students have learned how to "manipulate" the voice break in this way, they will sing songs more easily which ascend diatonically through the voice break.

The out-of-tune singer also profits from singing tonal echoes in a small ensemble with other students who are better singers. This better enables him to listen to, and concentrate on, his own singing. Further, the out-of-tune singer initially requires simple *harmonic* (not melodic) accompaniment (guitar, baritone ukulele, or piano) to these echo responses. It is much easier for an out-of-tune singer to develop a sense of tonality when listening to a "chording" instrument as he sings. If the piano is used for this purpose, to perform the melody is inappropriate. This is so because it provides the student an opportunity *not* to concentrate on his intonation because he can simply "follow" the piano as he might other students who continually sing with him. Moreover, it is more difficult for an out-of-tune singer to match tones played on a piano or xylophone than it is to match the human voice, and particularly that of another student. The use of a full piano accompaniment should be reserved until students have developed good tonal habits.

Larger intervals (such as perfect fourths and fifths based only on tonic functions and to a lesser extent, major and minor thirds and sixths based on all harmonic functions) should constitute tonal echo patterns. Major and minor seconds and sevenths and augmented and diminished intervals are, of course, harder to hear and as a result contribute little to the establishment of a sense of tonality. However, patterns which include the leading-tone (sung high) should be emphasized; the stress of the tonally active seventh step of the scale helps establish, through resolution, the concept of tonality. Consecutive repeated notes (unisons), slurs, and glissandos are not appropriate in echo patterns for these students. When a slide is made to a new pitch, a student tends *not* to think the pitch of the next note before he sings it, and as a result he sings out of tune because he has only an approximate idea of where the pitch should be placed. In short, the out-of-tune singer in this case will use his throat rather than his ear for pitch placement, and this will exaggerate his problem. Echo patterns, consisting of well-articulated staccato notes (separated but not short), are superior to legato passages for helping out-of-tune singers.

The discussion concerning the out-of-tune singer who lacks a sense of melodic direction is also relevant to an out-of-tune singer who lacks a sense of pitch. However, out-of-tune singers who have a sense of melodic direction may be allowed to sing echo responses that move in a similar melodic direction. Tonal syllable echoes particularly help this type of out-of-tune singer establish a sense of tonality. In addition, dialogue songs are useful because a singer who lacks a sense of pitch but not melodic direction is more able to deal with answers that lack exact melodic repetition.

There are students who are apparent nonsingers in the higher singing range but seem to sing in tune in the lower singing range. The explanation of this phenomenon is that this type of student is really a nonsinger; in the lower range, the student totally maximizes differences in pitch in his *speaking* voice. (However, it is difficult to sound precise pitches in a speaking voice even though one may differentiate among pitches in this range.) Although a student who behaves like a "combination" nonsinger and out-of-tune singer is sometimes erroneously considered to be in the process of a voice change, he truly is a nonsinger. After he develops his singing voice range, he will sing like an out-of-tune singer who lacks a sense of pitch.

Other Types

Students who sing in tune with a group but not individually have not developed the ability to listen and concentrate. They suffer the same limitations as out-of-tune singers with no sense of pitch, and their singing problems should be remedied accordingly. Students who can sing in tune individually but not with the group have generally been found to have a high degree of overall musical aptitude. They may profit from instrumental music lessons and other special musical activities.

ORGANIZATION OF TONAL PATTERNS

As alluded to earlier in this chapter, a sense of tonality comprises the ability to aurally perceive a resting tone within and among a pattern of pitches. And when a person establishes a vocabulary of various tonal patterns, it may be said that he has acquired the basis for musical enjoyment and understanding in the form of readiness to read and write tonal notation. The importance of perceiving and conceptualizing tonal patterns as a prelude to tonal reading has been discussed theoretically and investigated in experimental research studies. Recently Richards (58, 59) and Heffernan (27) have written methodological books based on this principle, and Thomas (70) has developed an extensive course of study which embodies the tenet. Probably the most extensive experimental research conducted on the subject has been accomplished by Petzold (53, 54, 55), DeYarman (15), Dittemore (16), and Langsford (40). Their results corroborate earlier theoretical discussions of Bean (5, 6) and Lowrey (43) and the more recent findings of Deutsch (14). Linton (42) even successfully developed a course of study for high school choral classes which emphasizes the intelligent perception of music as combinations of sound before the study of music theory and reading takes place.

Although there are only a few frequently used tonal patterns, there are, overall, conceivably more tonal patterns than rhythm patterns. Petzold (53) provides a complete description of tonal patterns in notational form in his monograph. In some situations, two or more tonal patterns may combine into a single pattern in the way upbeat patterns may combine with other rhythm patterns. Often a tonal pattern (*in notational form*) will comprise more than one rhythm pattern.

Tonal patterns generally include two or three tones; it is practically impossible to establish tonality with only one pitch and difficult to remember and apply patterns that include too many pitches. The more tones a pattern contains, the fewer times that exact pattern can be found in another piece of music. For example, a complete scale is not considered a tonal pattern because an intact scale is rarely found in songs or etudes.

Tonal patterns may be organized in the following manner: 1) Basic Major, 2) Basic Minor, 3) Uncommon Major, 4) Uncommon Minor, 5) Basic Modal, 6) Uncommon Modal, 7) Basic Unusual, and 8) Uncommon Unusual. The terms "basic" and "uncommon" refer simply to the frequency with which the patterns are found in music, the more numerous basic patterns being found more often. The terms "major" and "minor" like those of "modal" and "unusual," refer, of course, to type of tonality. However, in this connection, it should be understood that major and natural minor, theoretically speaking, correspond to the Ionic and Aeolian modes, respectively, and in practical usage they are referred to as the usual modes. Dorian, Phrygian, Lydian, and Mixolydian, because of their less frequent use, are referred to as the unusual modes.

The unusual modes can be recognized rather easily. The Dorian mode and the Phrygian mode are similar to the natural minor mode (Aeolian), the difference being that the Dorian mode has a raised sixth step and the Phrygian mode a lowered second step. Compared to the major mode, the Lydian mode has a raised fourth step and the Mixolydian mode a lowered seventh step. Harmonic minor is a variant of the Aeolian mode. Theoretically, every mode is based on a unique scale and therefore each has inimitable tonality. The letter name of the resting note of a mode is, of course, determined by the key signature. Patterns in unusual tonality bear no functional relationship to any of the modes and therefore the resting tone which they suggest is a matter of subjective opinion.

Basic major and minor patterns are primarily related to tonic, dominant and dominant seventh, and subdominant functions. Basic minor patterns are derived from harmonic minor. Naturally, some tonic patterns are closely related to mediant function, dominant and dominant seventh patterns to submediant function. Uncommon major and minor patterns include key-related chromatic intervals—those which do not necessarily act as embellishments but rather, generally relate to temporary modulations.

Basic modal patterns are those which are functions of Dorian, Phrygian, Lydian, and Mixolydian. Uncommon modal patterns are analogous to the appropriate basic and uncommon major and minor patterns as they function in the Pentatonic mode and the Hungarian (Gypsy) minor mode. Further, uncommon modal songs are comprised of combinations of basic modal patterns which give rise, for example, to the Dorian-Lydian mode.

Basic unusual patterns include nontonal chromatic embellishment intervals. Uncommon unusual patterns are analogous to the basic unusual patterns. However, when they are used extensively, they give rise to nontonal music. (Of course, nontonal music is also characterized through serial, triadic, pandiatonic, and polytonal techniques.)

TONAL READINESS

After the aural perception of tonal patterns is developed, the reading and writing of tonal notation are easily accomplished through the process of associating tonal patterns learned by rote with correlate notation. Rote tonal patterns are *not* best learned with *melodic rhythm* even when they are extracted from specific songs. If tonal patterns are learned with a specific melodic rhythm, application for reading purposes becomes restricted because tonal patterns are not usually found with the same melodic rhythm among different songs. Tonal patterns are better learned in a nondefinitive rhythm. In this way, rote tonal patterns can be applied for reading any song regardless of the specific melodic rhythm found with the tonal patterns in a given song. It should be emphasized that rote songs and recorded music, tonal chants, echoes, dialogues, rounds, rondos, and part songs serve well in developing a rote vocabulary of tonal patterns.

As suggested by DeYarman (15) and Dittemore (16), after students have established a rote vocabulary of tonic major and minor tonal patterns, they easily learn the remaining basic and uncommon major and minor patterns (those associated with dominant and subdominant functions) by rote. Next, the basic unusual and modal patterns, and later the uncommon modal and unusual patterns, are learned by rote. Students more easily learn to hear basic unusual patterns before basic modal patterns but uncommon modal patterns before uncommon unusual patterns.

Because major and minor music are emphasized in informal (out-of-school) activities, children are relatively unfamiliar with contemporary music. Therefore, they find it difficult to objectively identify a resting tone in unusual tonality and to sing and recall patterns in unusual tonality without first establishing a feeling for usual tonality. Usual tonality probably provides a basis for recognizing unusual tonality through a comparison of the familiar with the unfamiliar. This appears to be the case, but to a lesser extent, with uncommon modal tonality.

Some authorities, such as Orff (50), believe that young children should perform pentatonic music without half-steps, before music based on a diatonic scale. This probably is based on assumptions of early studies of scale development in ethnomusicology, which attempted to apply a theory of phylogeny (that we learn by systematically following the same process of that of mankind in general) as opposed to ontogeny (that we learn as individuals). Others—Coleman (13) and, more recently, Richards (59) who acknowledge the Kodály approach—support this point of view. It is reasoned that pentatonic music is superior because 1) it is easier to sing in that there are no half steps, 2) harmonic changes and traditional dissonance are eliminated, and 3) it can be easily performed on bell-type instruments. However, it is interesting to note that through systematic observation, Learned, Heliger, and Updegraff (41) found that preschool children sing spontaneously in the natural minor mode and in the Dorian mode. It would seem logical that when children enter school, they should continue to develop a sense of tonality by learning diatonic songs in major and minor with which they are at least informally acquainted, as well as those based on less familiar modes, versions of pentatonic, and nontonal music. Furthermore, songs which are based on a half step between the seventh and eighth steps of a scale facilitate the development of a feeling of tonality. It is for this reason that in presenting both major and minor songs to provide a basis for comparison of tonality, it is important that the harmonic form of minor be emphasized in early experiences. Songs written in the natural minor mode and in the unusual modes (Dorian, Phrygian, Lydian, and Mixolydian) should be learned more easily after students have developed a sense of tonality for the usual major and minor modes. As suggested, the development of an understanding of the "new" and "different" probably comes as a result of a comparison with the familiar and traditional.

Individual Differences in Tonal Readiness

Particularly in the work of Petzold (53, 54), Spohn (68), and Spohn and Whitney (67), the pronounced individual musical differences among students are quite obvious. Petzold's research was conducted with elementary school age students and Spohn and Whitney concentrated on college age students. Pflederer, even working with very young children, discovered that their responses to musical tasks embodying Piaget's principle of conservation were quite varied and that each child's musical understanding improved with appropriate training.

As in the case of rhythm, students' tonal readiness can be expected to develop in accordance with their tonal aptitudes. And, individual differences among students in regard to potential for developing tonal understandings may best be served within a *group situation*. For example, higher aptitude students are more able to perform more complex intervalic echo responses than lower aptitude students. Less gifted students can identify the tonality and resting tone of a song and are able to chant a simple tonal pattern as other students sing the song using the text.

Tonal dialogues and rondos contribute much to meeting the musical needs of individual students. For example, in preplanned and creative dialogues and rondos, more gifted students are capable of responding to a pattern in major with a parallel or relative sequence in minor, another mode, or in unusual tonality. Their responses might suggest a modulation or a return to the tonic when the pattern statement implies a temporary modulation, and their responses may purposely be based on a different harmonic sequence from that which was implied in the pattern. In general, high aptitude students are quite adept at improvisation. Finally, small groups of gifted students find it challenging to provide ensemble harmonic accompaniments to songs a class sings.

TONAL READING AND WRITING

Various techniques have been endorsed for teaching tonal reading readiness and tonal reading. Lundin (44) and Oakes (48) believe that "perfect pitch" is useful in this capacity. Kyme (39) has renewed interest in the shape note system for reading readiness purposes. Fuller (21) believes that a music notation system based on E and G would facilitate music reading ability, and Jones (35) has described the virtues of the tone-word approach of Carl Eitz for tonal reading. In their theoretical discussions, Bentley (7) and Heffernan (27) propose that the movable *do* system is superior to the fixed *do* system for reading readiness and reading purposes. Indirectly, Bentley concurs with Lowrey (43), Ortmann (52), and Van Nuys and Weaver (71) that factors of visual span and relativity of tones presuppose the importance of developing a tonal pattern vocabulary as a basis for music literacy.

From an analysis of the experimental research and philosophical writings pertaining to tonal literacy, it appears that tonal syllable patterns are superior for developing tonal reading readiness and tonal reading, particularly when compared to another popular technique, the number system. In the number system, the numbers 1 through 8 are used instead of *do, re, mi, fa, so, la, ti, do;* the raised tonal syllable accidentals are *di, ri, fi, si,* and *li* and the corresponding enharmonic lowered syllables are *ra, me, se, le,* and *te.*

There are some major disadvantages to the number system: 1) There is no provision for accidentals as there is in the tonal syllable system. Because of this limitation, chromatic patterns are usually not taught. If they are, numbers which are used for scale tones are also generally used for nonscale tones and this, of course, causes confusion on the part of students. 2) A minor scale is sung with a confounded number sequence of 6, 7, 8, 2, 3, 4, 5, 6, and not 1 through 8 because, according to the major scale, 2 to 3 represents a major second in sound. The second and third steps of a minor scale, of course, are separated by a minor second (a minor scale is sung from *la,* the tonic, to *la* with tonal syllables). 3) Students (particularly young ones) encounter difficulty when they have to skip numbers or sing numbers backwards, as dictated by melodic contour, and as an unfortunate result, readiness activities cannot be begun in the primary grades (in contrast, young students sing syllables with ease because there is no retroactive inhibition involved). 4) The number *seven* is a two-syllable word that creates rhythmic problems when sung; other numbers that include diphthongs also create difficulties when they are sung (tonal syllables consist of monosyllables without diphthongs). 5) Numbers end with harsh vowel sounds or consonants in contrast to the tonal syllables, which end in soft vowels that are more conducive to the production of good tone quality. 6) When melodies have a range greater than an octave, confusion arises because students are not sure whether to sing 2 or 9, for example; but with the tonal syllables, *re,* in this case, will be sung regardless. Nevertheless, numbers are very functional for explaining theoretical aspects of tonal notation *after* students are able to read music.

Other major advantages of tonal syllables, some of which are shared with other systems, follow: 1) Most importantly, after a tonal pattern is learned by rote, the relative pitch differences among syllables remain the same *regardless of key or mode.* 2) Easy transition can be made to relative major and minor keys. 3) Key signatures for any mode can be very easily interpreted. 4) Nontonal melodies can be easily read because C can always be thought of as *do,* as when singing in the system of fixed *do.*

The letter (pitch) name system (corresponding to the names of the lines and spaces of the staff) and the fixed *do* system are impractical because a given tonal pattern takes on different letters or syllables with a change of key. (When a student learns the relative sound of the tonal pattern *do, re, mi,* for example, he will recognize it and read it in any key or mode.) The processes of transfer and generalization are even more limited when the interval system approach is used for tonal reading, writing, and readiness because tonal patterns *are heard* in a tonic related context as opposed to an unrelated distance between a dyad. Furthermore, the ability to *name* an interval presupposes knowledge of note letter names and scales. (This in and of itself obviates the use of intervals with young children for readiness purposes). In addition, singing the name of an interval introduces many complex tonal and rhythmic problems.

A major disadvantage which the tonal syllable system shares with some other tonal reading approaches is that there are no syllables for a raised *mi* or lowered *do.* A common disadvantage shared by all systems is that a new resting tone must be sung if a song modulates to other than relative major or minor. Furthermore, as a result of the historical development of tonal syllables, there is an inherent illogic in the system. For the sake of consistency, *re* should really be called *ra* (like *fa* and *la*) and *ra* should really be called *re* (like *te, le, se,* and *me*).

As DeYarman (15) and Dittemore (16) indicate after students have established a rote *aural* vocabulary of tonic major and minor tonal syllable patterns, they are ready to learn to read and write these patterns in all functional keys. The concept that *do* and *la* can be either on a line or on a space of the staff, as established by the key signature, is difficult for students to understand. Before being directly exposed to tonal patterns in notational form, students profit from participating in a transitional activity. For example, the teachers' hand, with fingers apart, may serve as a staff; the fingers and thumb represent the lines and the area between them, the spaces. Any finger or space can be designated as *do* or *la.* Then by pointing with the other hand to appropriate lines and spaces, the teacher can quickly direct students in how to "read" tonal patterns. In this way, students logically comprehend the visual line-space relationship among tonal syllables as found in actual notation, and they easily develop a concept of the movable *do* system. Ultimately students learn that some tones are subordinate to others in the motion of the phrase toward tonal goals.

As in reading rhythm with rhythm syllables, students do not learn to read tonal notation by singing or *naming* the tonal syllables *from the beginning through the end of the song.* Rather, they learn to read tonal patterns just as they read in phrases in their spoken language. For consecutively repeated pitches, in a selected pattern, only one syllable should be sung. Generally, the first of two or more consecutively repeated pitches should end a tonal pattern and the next tonal pattern should begin with the syllable that corresponds to the next different pitch. Students read tonal notation by establishing an association between *tonal patterns* in notational form and correlate *tonal syllable patterns* learned by rote. Repetitions and sequences within and between songs become obvious. Songs are sung in entirety *using the text (not syllables)* because students sequentially learn to hear tonal patterns and connect them as phrases *by being aware of tonality* as they sing the words of the song.

Obviously, tonal syllables and rhythm syllables cannot be performed simultaneously. It seems probable that students learn to read rhythm and tonal patterns concurrently—primarily by observing first note stems, beams, and flags to deduce melodic rhythm and the note heads to discern melodic contour—as they sing the text of the song. After students have learned, and relearned if necessary, to read a pattern, syllables are *systematically abandoned* for that pattern. Tonal and rhythm syllables serve only as a basic *means* for learning to read patterns and do not represent an *end* in themselves.

As students are learning to read basic major and minor patterns that correspond to tonic functions (those patterns which were initially learned by rote), they concurrently rote learn and then read the remaining basic and uncommon major and minor tonal syllable patterns. Next, the basic unusual, basic modal, uncommon modal, and uncommon unusual patterns are learned by rote and then read.

When different key signatures are encountered, students learn the name of the key (C major or A minor, for example), and where *do* or *la* can be found on the staff. Through repetition (not memorization), students functionally learn the names of most, if not all, lines and spaces associated with the G clef and later with the F clef. In the same manner they also learn the names of many key signatures. Given proper tonal reading readiness, students will adequately read tonal patterns *without having to formally memorize the letter names of lines and spaces or of key signatures, or the order of sharps or flats as they appear in a key signature.* (In this connection it is interesting to reflect on the fact that for *singing* purposes, names of lines and spaces and key signatures need never be learned. If students understand only that the last sharp in a key signature is *ti* and the next to last flat is *do*, they can easily learn the function and location of the keynote.)

Tonal notation, like rhythm notation, should not be learned in an isolated way. Students best learn notational skills by writing tonal patterns (sung to them with tonal syllables or with neutral syllables) in more than one key or by writing those patterns performed for them on a melody instrument or heard on a recording. In this way, students may also learn to write patterns on the treble staff and the bass staff which are selected from familiar songs or specific responses to echoes and dialogues.

It is interesting to note that in the recent past there has been considerable research interest in improving students' ability to read musical notation through programmed learning and other audio-visual devices. Researchers are not unanimous as to whether programmed learning is efficient. As a result of their findings, Andrews (3), Sidnell (63), Spohn (68), and Spohn and Whitney (67) are enthusiastic proponents of the system, but Hewlett (28), Kanable (36), and Mandle (46) are less positive. Both Rea (57) and Stokes (69) found tachistoscopic training not to be more beneficial than traditional approaches in improving reading ability, although Hammer (24) reports positive results. Skapski (64), using synchronized video tapes and Hutton (31) visual aids, found them to be efficient in the instructional process.

Individual Differences in Tonal Reading and Writing

Research indicates that the individual differences among students in tonal aptitudes, as in readiness skills, should be taken into consideration when they are learning literacy skills. For example, as students with little aptitude perform echo responses, abler students are capable of notating those responses as well as specific preplanned responses. These students can be expected to write patterns from memory, whereas low aptitude students need to see and hear again what they write. More able students may notate patterns representing their creative (or improvised) dialogue responses as other students, in accordance with the complexity of the response, read these responses.

Initially, high aptitude students find it challenging to rewrite in minor tonality a pattern the class is learning to read in major tonality and vice versa. Similarly, these students are later able to transpose major, minor, and unusual modal patterns. They can create and improvise second and third parts to songs the class sings and then easily notate these accompaniments in various keys. Finally, these students rapidly learn to notate uncommon unusual tonal patterns.

THEORY OF TONAL NOTATION

Every key signature is given a letter name which corresponds to a name of a line or a space on the staff. The name of the line or space indicated by the key signature is *traditionally* given the name of *do*. In this sense, as Richards (59) points out, the key signature is not really a key signature but rather, a *"do signature"*—that is, it is the "key" for locating *do*. A key signature, in and of itself, does *not* indicate a key such as C major, A minor, D Dorian, etc. The key signature only indicates which, if any, pitches are to be raised (sharped) or lowered (flatted) in performance. A specific note becomes *do* by virtue of the fact that because certain pitches are raised or lowered (except, of course, when there are no sharps nor flats in the key signature), there develops a sequence of pitches separated by specific tonal intervals (theoretically called the scale) among which only one pitch can be *do*. Once this pitch is identified, we are able to study the music itself to determine the mode upon which the melody is based and from this mode, the key in which the music is written.

Actually, it is not relevant whether students learn to associate *la, re, do,* or any pitch with a key signature because what one needs to know to read a piece of music is its *tonality*. Once the tonality is determined, the name of the resting note (and key) can be easily identified. Consider the key signature of one sharp: if the tonality is major, then G *(do)* is the resting note; if the tonality is minor, then E *(la)* is the resting note; if the tonality is in an unusual mode such as Dorian, then A *(re)* is the resting note, etc. Ultimately, the performer must look beyond a key signature to frequently found tonal patterns or the final note to determine the tonality of a piece of music.

From the foregoing discussion of key signatures, it becomes obvious that key signatures have more relevance for instrumental music than for vocal music. An instrumentalist obviously must be concerned with which pitches must be raised or lowered as directed by the key signature. On the other hand, the vocalist will automatically sing the appropriate scale tones (if he has developed a sense of tonality) after he has determined the tonality of the song without necessarily being otherwise cognizant of the key signature. Instead of using a key signature to identify tonality and to locate *do,* a clef (or, as a matter of fact, any sign) could suffice for singing purposes.

Students best learn these and other theoretical concepts associated with tonal notation *after* they have developed facility in tonal reading. However, key signature names and note letter names need not be memorized in isolation. These technical facts should be functionally learned in a practical and interesting manner. For example, as described before for initial use with high ability young students, low ability older students are able to learn, in time, to read or rewrite a tonal pattern using a different key signature or to notate a major tonal pattern in minor, or vice versa.

Finally, in this connection, it should be mentioned that the terms "half step," "whole step," and "skip," in reference to tonal intervals, are adult abstractions. To the musically inexperienced students it only seems logical that the interval of a major second is a skip when compared with a minor second, in the same sense that a third or fourth is thought of as a skip. Similarly, as Hattwick (25) suggests, the terms "up," "down," "high," and "low," as they apply to melodic contour, are also abstractions. It is true that higher pitches are notated up on the staff but this is not obvious to the young listener. As a matter of fact, what is thought of as "up" by the adult may be "to the right-hand side" to an inexperienced student as he observes a performance at the piano. Students best interpret the meaning of these and other abstract terms, which are primarily associated with notation, only after they have developed proper readiness in the form of aural perception skills.

SUMMARY

A sense of tonality is fundamental to perceiving and conceptualizing musical sound. The ability to aurally perceive tonal patterns through musical imagery provides for basic musical enjoyment and understanding and constitutes tonal reading readiness.

A sense of tonality is efficiently developed by learning to sing. Through the use of appropriate remedial aids and knowledge of ranges, tessituras, and voice breaks, teachers can help the various types of poor singers adequately acquire tonal understanding. Regardless of their level of tonal aptitude, all students can learn how to sing. The extent to which they learn to sing with good intonation habits is, however, dependent on tonal aptitude.

Tonal patterns are learned most practicably when tonal syllables are used. Every tonal pattern is indigenous to either major, minor, or less familiar modes such as Dorian, Phrygian, Lydian, or Mixolydian. Unusual tonal patterns are found in nontonal music.

Instruction in tonal understanding is most beneficial when individual differences among students in tonal reading readiness and tonal reading are taken into account. The deficiencies of less capable students should be compensated for while the strengths of more able students are enhanced. All students can best learn the theory of tonal notation after they have learned to read tonal notation.

STUDY GUIDE

1. Explain how perceptual learning relates to the development of tonal understanding.
2. Explain how conceptual learning relates to the development of tonal understanding.
3. Explain what is meant by tonal readiness.
4. Explain what is meant by tonal literacy.

5. Explain how tonal readiness forms the basis of tonal literacy.
6. Why is tonal literacy so important to musical understanding?
7. Why does it take two or more pitches to establish tonality?
8. Discuss the comparative advantages and limitations of tonal syllables and numbers for learning to read tonal notation.
9. Explain the difference between a key signature and a *do* signature.
10. Develop a rationale for explaining to elementary school children why a key signature of one sharp does not necessarily signify the key of G major.
11. Define the terms "tessitura" and "voice break."
12. Explain the difference between a nonsinger and an out-of-tune singer.
13. Why do some authorities prefer to teach children songs based on the pentatonic scale before songs based on the diatonic scale?
14. Describe procedures that facilitate the transition from tonal reading readiness to tonal reading.
15. Explain how students concurrently read the rhythm, melody, and text of a song.

BIBLIOGRAPHY

1. Agnew, Marie, "A Comparison of Auditory Images of Children, Psychologists, and Musicians," *Psychology Review*, XXXI (1922), 268–78.

2. Alvin, Juliette, *Music for the Handicapped Child.* London: Oxford University Press, 1965.

3. Andrews, Austin, *Development and Trial of a Basic Course in Music Theory Using Self-Instructional Materials to Supplement Training Received in High School Performance Groups.* Washington, D.C.: Department of Health, Education, and Welfare. Office of Education, Bureau of Research. Ed. 018–112, 1967.

4. Andrews, Frances, and Ned Diehl, *Development of a Technique for Identifying Elementary School Children's Musical Concepts.* University Park: The Pennsylvania State University, 1967.

5. Bean, Kenneth L., "An Experimental Approach to the Reading of Music," *Psychological Monographs*, L (1938), 80.

6. Bean, Kenneth L., "Reading Music Instead of Spelling It," *Journal of Musicology*, I (1939), 1–5.

7. Bentley, Arnold, "Fixed or Movable Do," *Journal of Research in Music Education*, VII (1959), 163–68.

8. Bergan, John R., "The Relationship Among Pitch Identification, Imagery for Musical Sounds, and Musical Memory," *Journal of Research in Music Education*, XV (1967), 99–109.

9. Blyler, Dorothea, "The Song Choice of Children in the Elementary Grades," *Journal of Research in Music Education*, VIII (1960), 9–15.

10. Boardman, Eunice, "An Investigation of the Effect of Preschool Training on the Development of Vocal Accuracy in Young Children." Unpublished D.Ed. dissertation, University of Illinois, 1964.

11. Bridges, Virginia Ann, "An Exploratory Study of the Harmonic Discrimination Ability of Children in Kindergarten Through Grade Three in Two Selected Schools." Unpublished Ph.D. dissertation, The Ohio State University, 1965.

12. Burroughs, G. E. R., and J. N. Morris, "Factors Involved in Learning a Simple Musical Theme," *British Journal of Educational Psychology*, XXXII (1962), 18–28.

13. Coleman, Satis, *Creative Music for Children*. New York: G. P. Putnam's Sons, 1922.

14. Deutsch, Diana, "Music Recognition," *Psychological Review*, LXXVI (1969), 300–307.

15. DeYarman, Robert. "An Experimental Analysis of the Development of Rhythmic and Tonal Capabilities of Kindergarten and First Grade Children," Unpublished Ph.D. dissertation, University of Iowa, 1971.

16. Dittemore, Edgar, "An Investigation of Some Musical Capabilities of Elementary School Children." *Studies in the Psychology of Music*, VI (1970), 1–44.

17. Drexler, E. N., "A Study of the Ability to Carry a Melody at the Pre-School Level," *Child Development*, IX (1938), 319–32.

18. Edwards, Miriam H., "Tonal Thinking Objectives of Music Education in the Elementary School." Unpublished D.Ed. dissertation, University of California (Los Angeles), 1968.

19. Farnsworth, Paul, "Auditory Acuity and Musical Ability in the First Four Grades," *Journal of Psychology*, VI (1938), 95–98.

20. Fowler, Charles B., "Discovery Method: Its Relevance for Music Education," *Journal of Research in Music Education*, XIV (1966), 126–34.

21. Fuller, Carol M., "A Music Notation Based on E and G," *Journal of Research in Music Education*, XIV (1966), 193–96.

22. Gordon, Kate, "Some Tests on the Memorizing of Musical Themes," *Journal of Experimental Psychology*, II (1917), 93–99.

23. Gould, A. Oren, "The Development of Specialized Programs for Singing in the Elementary School," *Council for Research in Music Education*, VI (1965), 17–24.

24. Hammer, Harry, "An Experimental Study of the Use of the Tachistoscope in the Teaching of Melodic Sight Singing," *Journal of Research in Music Education*, XI (1963), 44–54.

25. Hattwick, Melvin S., and H. M. Williams, *A Genetic Study of Differential Pitch Sensitivity*. Volume 2, *Iowa Studies in Child Welfare*. Iowa City: University of Iowa, 1935.

26. Hattwick, Melvin S., "The Role of Pitch Level and Pitch Range in the Singing of School Children," *Child Development*, IV (1933), 281–91.

27. Heffernan, Charles W., *Teaching Children to Read Music*. New York: Appleton-Century-Crofts, 1968.

28. Hewlett, Rex J., "An Investigation of the Effectiveness of Two Methods of Student Response Using a Taped Program of Practice Materials for Improving Aural Discrimination." Unpublished Ph.D. dissertation, Michigan State University, 1966.

29. Hewson, Alfred T., "Music Reading in the Classroom," *Journal of Research in Music Education*, XIV (1966), 289–302.

30. Hissem, Irene, "A New Approach to Music for Young Children," *Child Development*, IV (1933), 309–17.

31. Hutton, Doris, "A Comparative Study of Two Methods of Teaching Sight Singing in the Fourth Grade," *Journal of Research in Music Education*, I (1953), 119–26.

32. Jeffries, Thomas B., "The Effects of Order of Presentation and Knowledge of Results on the Aural Recognition of Melodic Intervals," *Journal of Research in Music Education*, XV (1967), 179–90.

33. Jersild Arthur, and Sylvia Bienstock, "A Study of the Development of Children's Ability to Sing," *Journal of Education Psychology*, XXV (1934), 281–503.

34. Jersild, Arthur, and Sylvia Bienstock, "The Influence of Training on the Vocal Ability of Three Year Old Children," *Child Development*, II (1931), 272–91.

35. Jones, Arnold, "The Tone-Word System of Carl Eitz," *Journal of Research in Music Education*, II (1966), 84–98.

36. Kanable, Betty, "An Experimental Study Comparing Programmed Instruction with Classroom Teaching of Sightsinging," *Journal of Research in Music Education*, XVII (1969), 217–26.

37. King, Harry, "A Study of the Relationship of Music Reading and I.Q. Scores," *Journal of Research in Music Education*, II (1954), 35–37.

38. Kirkpatrick, William C., "Relationships Between the Singing Ability of Pre-Kindergarten Children and Their Home Musical Environment." Unpublished D.Ed. dissertation, University of Southern California, 1962.

39. Kyme, George, "An Experiment in Teaching Children to Read Music with Shape Notes," *Journal of Research in Music Education,* VIII (1960), 3–8.

40. Langsford, Henry Marble, "An Experimental Study of the Effect of Practice upon Improvement in Melodic Dictation." Unpublished Ph.D. dissertation, Michigan State University, 1959.

41. Learned, Janet, D. Heliger, and Ruth Updegraff, "The Effect of Training upon Singing Ability and Musical Interest of Three, Four, and Five-Year Old Children," *University of Iowa Studies in Child Welfare,* XIV (1938), 83–131.

42. Linton, Stanley, *The Development of a Planned Program for Teaching Musicians in the High School Choral Class.* Washington, D.C.: Department of Health, Education, and Welfare. Office of Education, Bureau of Research. Ed. 126–402, 1967.

43. Lowery, H., "On Reading Music," *Dioptrical Review and British Journal of Physiological Optics,* I (1940), 78–88.

44. Lundin, Robert W., "Can Perfect Pitch Be Learned," *Music Educators Journal,* XLIX (1963), 49–51.

45. Mainwaring, James, "Psychological Factors in the Teaching of Music," *British Journal of Educational Psychology,* XXI (1951), 105–21, 199–213.

46. Mandle, William D., *A Comparative Study of Programmed and Traditional Technique for Teaching Music Reading in the Upper Elementary Schools Utilizing a Keyboard Approach.* Washington, D.C.: Department of Health, Education, and Welfare. Office of Education, Bureau of Research. Ed. 014–212, 1967.

47. Movsesian, Edwin, "The Influence of Teaching Music Reading Skills on the Development of Basic Reading Skills in the Primary Grades." Unpublished D.Ed. dissertation, University of Southern California, 1967.

48. Oakes, W. F., "An Experimental Study of Pitch Naming and Pitch Discrimination Reactions," *Journal of Genetic Psychology,* LXXXVI (1955), 237–59.

49. Olson, Rees Garn, "A Comparison of Two Pedagogical Approaches Adapted to the Acquisition of Melodic Sensitivity in Sixth Grade Children: The Orff Method and the Traditional Method." Unpublished D.Ed. dissertation, Indiana University, 1964.

50. Orff, Carl, *Music for Children.* New York: Associated Music Publishers, 1956.

51. Ortmann, Otto, "On the Melodic Relativity of Tones," *Psychological Monographs,* XXXV (1926), 1–47.

52. Ortmann, Otto, "Span of Vision in Note Reading," *Yearbook of the Music Supervisors National Conference* (1937), 88–93.

53. Petzold, Robert, *Auditory Perception of Musical Sounds by Children in the First Six Grades.* Madison: University of Wisconsin, 1966.

54. Petzold, Robert, "The Development of Auditory Perception of Musical Sounds by Children in the First Six Grades," *Journal of Research in Music Education,* XI (1963), 21–43.

55. Petzold, Robert, "The Perception of Music Symbols in Music Reading by Normal Children and by Children Gifted Musically," *Journal of Experimental Education,* XXVIII (1960), 271–319.

56. Pflederer, Marilyn, "The Responses of Children to Musical Tasks Embodying Piaget's Principle of Conservation," *Journal of Research in Music Education,* XII (1964), 251–68.

57. Rea, Ralph C., "Music Reading Films," *Journal of Research in Music Education,* II (1954), 112–20.

58. Richards, Mary Helen, *The Fourth Year.* Palo Alto: Fearon Publishers, 1966.

59. Richards, Mary Helen, *Threshold to Music.* Palo Alto: Fearon Publishers, 1964.

60. Ritchie, Tom Vernon, "A Study of the Effects of Diatonic Harmony upon the Aural Perception of Selected Melodic Fragments." Unpublished D.Ed. dissertation, Indiana University, 1960.

61. Sears, Margaret, "The Tape Recorder Employed in the Development of Children's Singing: An Experimental Study," *Colorado Journal of Research in Music Education,* II (1965), 8–12.

62. Sherman, Robert W., and Robert E. Hill, *Aural and Visual Perception of Melody in Tonal and Atonal Musical Environments.* Washington, D.C.: Department of Health, Education, and Welfare. Office of Education, Bureau of Research. Ed. 123–340, 1967.

63. Sidnell, Robert G., *The Development of Self-Instructional Drill Materials to Facilitate the Growth of Score Reading Skills of Student Conductors.* Washington, D.C.: Department of Health, Education, and Welfare. Office of Education Bureau of Research. Ed. 023–344, 1968.

64. Skapski, George S., *Feasibility of Producing Synchronized Video Tapes as Instructional Aids in the Study of Music.* Washington, D.C.: Department of Health, Education, and Welfare. Office of Education, Bureau of Research. Ed. 030–313, 1969.

65. Smith, E., "The Value of Notated Examples in Learning to Recognize Musical Themes Aurally," *Journal of Research in Music Education,* I (1953), 97–104.

66. Smith, Robert, "The Effects of Group Vocal Training on the Singing Ability of Nursery School Children," *Journal of Research in Music Education,* XI (1963), 137–41.

67. Spohn, Charles L., and Ransom D. Whitney, *Diagnosing and Correcting Individual Deficiencies in Learning Music.* Washington, D.C.: Department of Health, Education, and Welfare. Office of Education, Bureau of Research. Ed. 019–292, 1968.

68. Spohn, Charles L., "An Exploration in the Use of Recorded Teaching Material to Develop Aural Comprehension in College Music Classes," *Journal of Research in Music Education,* X (1963), 91–98.

69. Stokes, Charles F., "An Experimental Study of Tachistoscopic Training in Reading Music." Unpublished D.Ed. dissertation, University of Cincinnati, 1944.

70. Thomas, Ronald, *A Study of New Concepts, Procedures, and Achievements in Music Learning as Developed in Selected Music Education Programs.* Washington, D.C.: Department of Health, Education, and Welfare. Office of Education, Bureau of Research. Ed. 003–126, 1966.

71. Van Nuys, K., and H. E. Weaver, "Memory Span and Visual Pauses in Reading Rhythms and Melodies," *Psychological Monographs,* LV (1943), 33–50.

72. Williams, H. M., "Immediate and Delayed Memory of Pre-school Children for Pitch in Tonal Sequences," *University of Iowa Studies in Child Welfare,* XI (1935), 85–95.

73. Wunderlich, Henry, "Four Theories of Tonality," *Journal of Musicality,* II (1941), 171–80.

74. Wunderlich, Henry, "Theories of Tonality," *Journal of Genetic Psychology,* XXXVII (1947), 169–76.

CHAPTER SEVEN

listening

Probably because of past educational practices, the term "music appreciation" has been closely allied, by professional musicians and the lay public alike, with passive listening to music for the purpose of sensuous enjoyment. Actually, when a person has achieved music appreciation, he aesthetically enjoys listening to music because he understands, through aural perception and conceptualization, the tonal and rhythmic aspects, timbre, formal structure, and stylistic elements of the music to which he is listening. In this sense, music appreciation is a broad term that includes much more than just idly listening to music. Specifically, comprehensive music appreciation includes, and is contingent on music appreciation readiness—on an aural and kinesthetic *understanding* of the tonal and rhythmic aspects of music. And music appreciation readiness is systematically developed through discriminative listening to "live" as well as recorded music.

To appreciate English literature, one must understand the English language. It is true that a child could derive sensuous enjoyment from hearing a language spoken even though he might not understand the meaning of the words he hears. However, to more fully appreciate English literature, a person must conceive, as well as perceive, what he hears. Precisely for this reason very young children are generally not exposed to Shakespeare. Likewise, a child may revel in the sheer sound of music without an understanding of what he hears. But without appropriate preparation it is frivolous to expect a very young child to conceptualize, with aesthetic sophistication, the major works of Bach, Beethoven, Mozart, and Bartok, or the improvisations of progressive jazz artists. It is axiomatic that to expose students to great works of art without proper readiness represents inefficient procedures, which in time can transform wishful and unrealistic thinking on the part of the teacher into negative attitudes on the part of frustrated students.

When compared to other aspects of music education, there is relatively little experimental research evidence which bears on the value of, and the procedures for, music listening. The available evidence suggests that passive listening to music is an inefficient technique for teaching students to enjoy music, if teaching one to enjoy music can be accomplished at all. Although Crickmore (7) found that students of college age can listen restfully to music and derive enjoyment on five plateaus, Barrett (3), Colwell (6), and Duerksen (9), dealing with students of all ages, are of a mind to believe that passive listening to music in no way contributes to enjoyment. As a matter of fact, on the basis of their findings, Colwell stressed the idea that students need substantial musical training to begin to learn how to intelligently enjoy music. Duerksen admonishes music teachers to revise their goals pertaining to effects of passive listening or to completely eliminate the activity from the curriculum. Fitzpatrick (11) alludes to the importance of readiness training for the enjoyment of music; his research implies that only after students of high school age receive concentrated training in aurally perceiving and conceptualizing music can they react in a significant manner to melody, form, structure, texture, and tone color. Bailey (2) and Routch (16) have developed tests to measure these understandings.

According to students' introspective analyses and objective evaluations of teachers (using student interest as a criterion), it appears that students can be made to indicate a preference for music which they have passively listened to over and over again. The research of Bridges (5), Evans (10), Getz (13), and Hornyak (15) supports this notion. To the extent that one wishes to believe that forced preference on the part of students is a worthwhile objective, it should be remembered that, as Evans clearly points out, musical preference does not presuppose musical understanding. Duerksen (8), in another study, gives credibility to this conclusion when he states that he found no practical relationship between students' preference for a piece of music and their intelligent musical understanding of that composition. This was true even for students who had musical training.

In view of these findings, researchers in the last decade have, nevertheless, attempted to discover new techniques for teaching children to enjoy music through passive listening. Andrews (1) compared the efficacy of student self-initiated instruction to that of traditional teacher dominated instruction; Fullard (12) experimented with programmed operant training with preschool children; Haack (14) contrasted the inductive and deductive approaches; and Seipp (17) experimented with the effect of order of presentation. None found any positive results, although Andrews demonstrated that when left to their own devices, students develop better attitudes about listening to music.

One of the most interesting studies, and one of the earliest, is that of Belaiew-Exemplarsky. While she makes no pretense that students necessarily enjoy passive listening to music, she does emphasize in her findings that they tend to like music which comprises timbre and dynamic contrasts and pronounced rhythmic elements.

MUSIC APPRECIATION AND READINESS

The term "appreciation" connotes both understanding and enjoyment. From a résumé of the research literature, it appears that to truly appreciate music, one must first understand what he hears so that he can fully enjoy it. Mere listening to music does not elicit intelligent musical enjoyment, but listening with understanding can foster musical enjoyment. And, as Duerksen (9) indicates, it should be emphasized that musical understanding does not necessarily beget musical enjoyment, although we tend to enjoy what we understand.

Students learn to appreciate music through the developmental process of learning to understand music. As students achieve in music, they continuously develop an understanding of music. Achievement in music constitutes a systematic study of tonal and rhythmic elements, timbre, musical form, and musical style. Singing and rhythmic activities, creativity, the reading and writing of music, and *listening* to music, one and all, represent facets of musical achievement which contribute to music understanding. This understanding, through achievement, provides the *readiness* for music appreciation. Students can be expected to learn to understand and enjoy some types of music, and to understand but not enjoy other types of music. The responsibility of music educators is to teach students to understand all types of music so that students will have been provided with the proper readiness to appreciate (enjoy as well as understand) music of their own choosing. To simply tell students what is good music or bad music or what type of music they should like (even if the criterion is something other than the personal preference of the teacher) is becoming increasingly difficult to endorse as sound educational practice.

When listening to music is used as a method of providing music appreciation readiness, research results suggest that it should be of the active type, and not the passive type, which forces students to be quiet, listen, and to "appreciate." Students should be given the opportunity to listen to all types of music as a readiness procedure, but for most efficient and beneficial results they should be guided in actively responding to music to which they are listening. For example, as they are being exposed to any type of music, students can be directed to determine the tonality and meter of the music, to engage in eurhythmic activities with the music, to perform rhythmic and tonal accompaniments on instruments, to recognize specific tonal and rhythmic patterns, to listen for modulation and meter changes, to determine harmonic structure, to create an additional melodic part or a rhythmic ostinato, to notate recurring tonal and rhythmic patterns, or to read the notation of the music. All of these activities contribute to the development of tonal and rhythmic perception and conception (as described in previous chapters), which in turn establish music appreciation readiness. To ask students only to listen for programmatic implications of music or to recognize the sound of specific instruments provides them precious little readiness for coping with the spectrum of comprehensive music appreciation.

Colwell (6) alludes to the fact that allotted music periods are too short in elementary schools to allow for adequate instruction in musical form and style. However, it is possible that the elementary school age students whom he studied did not profit from such instruction because they did not possess the proper appreciation readiness. Too, because the attention span of young students is relatively short, it was probably difficult for them to sit quietly and concentrate on sophisticated complexity in music. It would seem that if elementary school age students were provided with proper music appreciation readiness, they would be more able to deal with aspects of musical form and style in the middle or junior high school, where music periods are somewhat longer. Moreover, it is interesting to ponder how much more pleasurable the teaching and learning of musical form and style in the upper grades could be if students actually developed appreciation skills through perceptional and conceptional processes in elementary school. Instead of verbally explaining form, for example, the teacher could direct students to listen aesthetically for a modulation which heralds a second theme in the exposition, or for fragments of a theme or the recurrence of a theme in different rhythms in the development section of a composition in sonata form. Or, what could be more advantageous for a student than to possess the necessary understanding for writing his own composition in the style of a renowned composer in an attempt to discern and compare, and ultimately appreciate, musical style. Suffice it to say that in the pursuit of music appreciation an *understanding of* music is of comparatively more value than *knowing about* music.

SUMMARY

Music appreciation comprises both musical understanding and musical enjoyment. Musical understanding, derived through musical achievement, is basic to musical enjoyment. In this sense, musical achievement constitutes the readiness for music appreciation.

Mere listening to music does not necessarily signify that music appreciation is taking place. Learning to listen to music in an active way is one of many techniques, including singing, eurhythmic, literacy, and creative activities, which provide for music appreciation readiness. After a student acquires music appreciation readiness, he is better able to profit from listening to music for the purpose of enjoyment. And when a student can passively listen to music with understanding and enjoyment, he may be considered to possess a comprehensive appreciation of music.

STUDY GUIDE

1. Define the term "music appreciation."
2. Differentiate between musical enjoyment and understanding.
3. Explain the difference between actively and passively listening to music.
4. Describe what is meant by music appreciation readiness.
5. When a young child actively listens to another child sing or to his teacher sing, is he developing music appreciation readiness in the same sense as he does when he actively listens to a recording?
6. Try to explain why institutions of higher learning offer courses in music appreciation and art appreciation, although courses in physical science appreciation or social studies appreciation, for example, are not listed in the college catalogue.

BIBLIOGRAPHY

1. Andrews, Dorothy, "A Comparative Study of Two Methods of Developing Music Listening Ability in Elementary School Children," *Journal of Research in Music Education,* X (1962), 59–68.

2. Bailey, Ben, "The Development and Validation of a Test of Listening Skill," *Journal of Research in Music Education,* XVI (1968), 59–63.

3. Barrett, Roger Lee, "A Study of the General Nature of Ideational Perception in Music." Unpublished Ph.D. dissertation, University of Iowa, 1961.

4. Belaiew-Exemplarsky, Sophie, "Das musikalische Empfinden im Vorschulealter," *Zeischrift für angewandte Psychologie,* XXVII (1926), 177–216.

5. Bridges, Virginia Ann, "An Exploratory Study of the Harmonic Discrimination Ability of Children in Kindergarten Through Grade Three in Two Selected Schools." Unpublished Ph.D. dissertation, Ohio State University, 1965.

6. Colwell, Richard, *Theory of Expectation Applied to Music Listening.* Department of Health, Education, and Welfare. Washington, D.C.: Office of Education, Bureau of Research. Ed. 010–040, 1966.

7. Crickmore, Leon, "An Approach to the Measurement of Music Appreciation," *Journal of Research in Music Education,* XVI (1968), 239–53.

8. Duerksen, George L., "A Study of the Relationship Between the Perception of Musical Processes and Musical Enjoyment," *Council for Research in Music Education,* XII (1968), 1–8.

9. Duerksen, George L., "Recognition of Repeated and Altered Thematic Materials in Music," *Journal of Research in Music Education,* XVI (1968), 3–30.

10. Evans, Jesse Gillette, "The Effect of Especially Designed Music Listening Experiences on Junior High School Students' Attitudes Toward Music." Unpublished D.Ed. dissertation, Indiana University, 1965.

11. Fitzpatrick, James B., "The Development and Evaluation of a Curriculum in Music Listening Skills on the Seventh Grade Level." Unpublished Ph.D. dissertation, University of Iowa, 1968.

12. Fullard, William G., "Operant Training of Aural Musical Discrimination with Preschool Children," *Journal of Research in Music Education,* XV (1967), 201–9.

13. Getz, Russell P., "The Effects of Repetition on Listening Response," *Journal of Research in Music Education,* XIV (1966), 178–92.

14. Haack, Paul, "A Study in the Development of Music Listening Skills of Secondary School Students," *Journal of Research in Music Education,* XVII (1969), 205–16.

15. Hornyak, Roy Robert, "A Factor Analysis of the Relationships Between the Components of Music Present in Selected Musical Examples and Preference Rating Responses of College Students to the Selected Musical Examples." Unpublished D.Ed. dissertation, Indiana University, 1964.

16. Routch, William Valgence, "The Construction and Validation of an Achievement Test in Music Appreciation for General College Students in State Teachers Colleges of Pennsylvania." Unpublished D.Ed. dissertation, The Pennsylvania State University, 1957.

17. Seipp, Kenneth F., "An Exploratory Study in Music Appreciation: A Comparison of the Effectiveness of Two Different Orders of Presentation upon Post-Instructional Retention." Unpublished D.Ed. dissertation, Indiana University, 1963.

18. Topp, Gordon D., "Recorded Music Recommended for Teaching Music Appreciation in Elementary Schools." Unpublished Ph.D. dissertation, University of Michigan, 1967.

CHAPTER
EIGHT

instrumental music

INSTRUMENTAL MUSIC READINESS

Ostensibly, participation in school music group instrumental activities ultimately depends on ability to read music. Realistically, to read instrumental music properly, one must be able to hear tonally and feel rhythmically what is seen in music notation before it is performed on a musical instrument. A student may memorize and spell the letter names and values of notes and then associate them with keys or valves on a wind instrument or with positions on the keyboard of a stringed instrument. This theoretical knowledge does not really constitute the ability to comprehend instrumental notation musically any more than does the ability to manipulate a typewriter keyboard mechanically presuppose cognition of what is being typed. By accurately hearing tonal patterns which are seen in notational form, a wind player is able to compensate for the mechanical imperfection of his instrument and, as Yarborough (46) suggests, a young string player is able to adjust his fingers kinesthetically on the keyboard. As a result of his ability to aurally image the musical patterns seen in notational form, an instrumentalist is better able to perform in tune both in solo and, especially, in ensemble. Similarly, with regard to rhythm, a more musical performance results if one is able to hear patterns and anticipate rhythm as it *interacts with tonal elements* because then he need not try to calculate the value of each note simultaneously with sound production. In this sense, Gordon (14) believes that one is always "sightreading," at least until he has memorized and no longer reads a given piece of music.

When a student demonstrates a sense of tonality and meter, it can be assumed that he has established a rote vocabulary of frequently heard tonal and rhythm patterns. A student should learn to recognize these patterns in notational form (as described in Chapters Five and Six) before he attempts to learn to manipulate a musical instrument technically. In his research, Noble (30) stresses the value of this type of development for successful instrumental performance.

There is no correct chronological age for a student to begin taking instrumental music lessons. The proper time for a student to begin instrumental music instruction is just as soon as he demonstrates musical readiness for studying an instrument—specifically, *after* he can sing in tune and perform with stability of tempo and a sense of meter. Fred (11) found that to learn instrumental and vocal music concurrently was in no way conducive to learning to perform better in tune. If a student demonstrates a sense of tonality and meter in accordance with his levels of corresponding aptitude and has developed tonal and rhythm pattern vocabulary readiness, *then* extra-musical factors, such as interest in studying an instrument and physical coordination ability, also become of importance in decision making. It would not make sense to force a student to take instrumental lessons or to expect a student to execute intricate fingering patterns if he lacks the requisite physical control. As a matter of fact, Cramer (7) found that success in beginning instrumental music was significantly related to motor development but not to physical growth or chronological age. Much earlier, Colby (5) came to the same conclusion regarding children three to four years old. Cramer (7) suggests that the optimum time to start instrumental training is in the seventh grade or later. Nelson (28, 29) concluded that it is uneconomical to begin instrumental instruction with students (unless possibly they are in the genius class) until they are at least in the fifth grade. But the fact still remains that regardless of dexterity, maturation, or age, prime consideration should be given to music readiness when considering a student for instruction in instrumental music.

INSTRUMENTAL MUSIC INSTRUCTION

Generally speaking, emphasis is placed on tonal understanding in instrumental music instruction. The teacher is typically more concerned about whether the student plays the "right note" (pitch) than he is about rhythmic correctness. This, as implied by Yarborough (46), probably is a result of a preoccupation with associating letter names of notes with fingering. To develop adequate rhythm understanding, Froseth (12) has suggested that students first perform on rhythm instruments (to learn to interpret rhythm notation through another medium in addition to their voices) before they read two-dimensional (tonal and rhythm) instrumental notation. That this is more important than might be apparent is evidenced by the fact that so many instrumental students tap their feet while performing. Particularly, when this occurs with young students, it can be assumed that they lack the necessary eurhythmic feeling (readiness) for interpreting rhythm notation and as a result they are still quite dependent on overt rhythmical response. Evidence of another type which suggests that many instrumental students lack rhythm readiness for instrumental performance is that they generally enter early, and sometimes late, after a notational rest. No doubt these students "count" tempo beats during rests, but obviously they are not feeling tempo beats with sufficient stability. The credibility of the foregoing ideas might best be supported by acknowledging the favor those students (as well as adults) who lack rhythm readiness bestow on popular music. The tempo beats in this type of music are so pronounced that they compensate for one's inability to organize rhythmic factors without obvious and persistent external direction.

By and large, literature for beginning instrumental students utilizes more than one meter signature for music in duple meter and, likewise, for music in triple meter. For purposes already explained in Chapter Five, young instrumentalists will learn literacy skills more efficiently if the number of meter signatures to which they are exposed is initially limited. And in this connection it would seem that if beginning methods books are used, those which emphasize "shorter" notes (as they function in rhythm patterns), and not whole or half notes, are more appropriate. While it might be true that "long" tones aid in the development of breath control and good tone quality, these attributes are not best acquired at the expense of rhythmic understanding. Certainly proper breath control can be developed and good tone quality can be established in ways which will not sacrifice rhythmic understanding. Finally, in regard to rhythm, it appears to be perfunctory for instrumentalists to *sequentially* "count" tempo beats, as they apply to the upper number of a meter signature, while performing music. Students better "keep their place" by feeling tempo and meter and relating to rhythm patterns, than by performing a function akin to that of an adding machine.

Ideally, if a student displays proper musical readiness he should be given an opportunity to study instrumental music if he so desires. Students who possess higher levels of musical aptitude are properly encouraged to participate in performing groups, but this does not mean that others need be excluded. The research results of Froseth (12) and Gordon (14) indicate that regardless of his degree of aptitude, any student can profit from instrumental music instruction just as soon as he has developed the music readiness which can reasonably be expected from knowledge of his levels of musical aptitude. While it is true that private lessons are beneficial for students who have developed considerable facility on an instrument, Waa (44) has demonstrated that ensemble instruction (either of the heterogeneous or like-instrument type) is most conducive for developing musical understanding for beginning students. Specifically, to play in tune is, in the most practical sense, ultimately a matter of playing in tune in ensemble; and to play rhythmically is really a matter of being sensitive to the practice of others as dictated by the music. When playing alone, these learning opportunities are not as well accorded as in ensemble performance, although it is possible that technical facility might be learned more quickly through private instruction. Probably more importantly, as Hatfield (16) found, when literature is performed musically, many contingent problems of technique are mitigated.

Beginning instrumental students quickly develop a familiarity with their instrument, enhance their tonal and rhythmic understanding, and maintain an interest in instrumental music if they are given immediate opportunity to improvise on their instruments (particularly before they are formally taught to read instrumental notation). The research of Froseth (12), Gordon (14), Luce (25), and Suzuki (42) supports this belief. The simplest and most efficient methods for developing improvisational ability are through instrumental echo and dialogue techniques and by the rote performance of simple tunes learned in general music classes.

The use of echo and dialogue techniques in general music classes to provide instruction that meets the individual musical needs of students has been discussed in Chapters Five and Six. These techniques are easily adaptable to similar objectives in instrumental music instruction. In some cases, they may be used as an introduction to, or as an extension of, instrumental performance. Froseth (12) and Hatfield (16) provide material in notational form and suggestions for adapting existent literature to serve these purposes.

After the identification of talented students to participate in instrumental activities, the most important educational responsibility of the instrumental teacher, according to Froseth (12), Gordon (13, 14), and Hatfield (16), is to teach to the *individual musical differences* among students after they have become participants in a performance group. This is particularly relevant for students of average and low musical aptitude. Not only do students differ from *one another* (normatively) in musical aptitudes, but, as heretofore stressed, the level of each dimension of a student's musical aptitude is generally found to be different when he is "compared" to *himself* (idiographically).

RELATED FACTORS

    Studies which have primary relevance to method and technique, as they apply to instrumental music, are quite numerous in the literature of the psychology of music. Because some of these investigations bear on the sequential manner in which instrumental music learning develops, they will be briefly discussed.

    Efficiency in memorizing music was first experimentally investigated by Eberly and later reported by Rubin-Rabson (34). It was found that when a piano composition was studied as a whole, students learned to memorize it faster than when it was studied in parts. Brown (3) also investigated a combination of the whole and part method and still found the whole method approach most effective. Rather than have students demonstrate retention through instrumental performance, after two weeks Rubin-Rabson (35) had them transcribe in notational form what they had learned. She found no superiority for either the whole or the part method. On the contrary, O'Brien (31) derived results which favored the part method. Obviously, the results of these (and the following) investigations were largely related to experimental design.

    Juhacy (20) and Kovacz (22) investigated whether analytical prestudy away from the keyboard benefited learning and agreed that it is most useful. They also stated that musical memory is developed through musical imagery. Rubin-Rabson (37, 41) compared the efficacy of various types of prestudy to none at all. She found a marked improvement in performance as a result of prestudy, regardless of type, and that longer prestudy periods proved to be most conducive to learning. However, hearing music performed before it was studied did not aid students in the memorization of compositions. In a related study, Rubin-Rabson (38) reported that mental rehearsal, either before or after learning, is inferior to that done midway as music is being learned.

    Rubin-Rabson (32, 39) also investigated the effect of different degrees of overlearning on the memorization of keyboard music. Students continued to practice half as many times (fifty percent overlearning), as many times again (one hundred percent overlearning), and one and a half as many times (one hundred fifty percent overlearning) as it took them to initially memorize a given composition. No degree of overlearning was found to be more effective for retention than any other, although any degree was more effective than none at all. Becker (2), working with junior high school cornet and trumpet players, ostensibly came to the same conclusion.

In regard to the memorization of piano music, Rubin-Rabson (34) found that neither massed (all at once) nor distributed (over time) practice was superior. However, for purposes of relearning, distributed practice proved to be more efficient, especially for less able students. Practicing hands alone (the unilateral approach) and hands together (the coordinated approach) produce different results in regard to speed in learning piano music. Rubin-Rabson (33) and Brown (3) agree that the coordinated approach is most efficient.

Negative practice (that is, the purposeful practice of errors as an aid in eliminating those errors) has not been found fruitful for musical learning. Neither Wakeham (45) nor Johnson (19) support the beta hypothesis. In regard to offering a cash reward to increase speed in learning, Rubin-Rabson (36) found this incentive to be of no avail.

DiFronzo (9) and Diamond and Sorel (8), in their research on the efficacy of using the tachistoscope to improve instrumental music sight reading, concluded that it produces superior results when contrasted with conventional methods. In his evaluation of electronic self-instruction, Lund (26) demonstrated that a programmed approach is quite beneficial in developing music reading skill at the piano keyboard. And Gutsch (15) believes he has developed a valid test of evaluating the individual student's instrumental music performance ability.

SUMMARY

Participation in school music group instrumental activities ultimately depends on the ability to read music. Realistically, to read instrumental music properly, one must be able to hear tonally and feel rhythmically what is seen in musical notation before it is performed on a musical instrument. Instrumental music readiness, then, in the form of a developed sense of tonality and meter and of an established vocabulary of tonal and rhythmic patterns, must be developed before a student can be expected to learn to perform well on a musical instrument.

In general, students learn to play an instrument more easily by participating in ensemble activities than by simply taking private lessons and participating in large performance groups. In small group lessons, students benefit from learning to improvise on their instruments before they are formally taught sophisticated technique or how to read instrumental music notation.

All students, regardless of their levels of musical aptitude, can profit from instrumental music instruction. Musical aptitude test results should be used not only for identifying talented students but, more importantly, for teaching to talented and less able students' individual musical differences, both normatively and idiographically.

STUDY GUIDE

1. Explain what is meant by instrumental music readiness.
2. Describe why improvisational ability is so important to successful instrumental music performance.
3. Why do you think small group lessons might be more practicable than private lessons?
4. Develop a definition of the term "sightreading."
5. React to the following statement. "There is a higher correlation between instrumental music reading ability and academic intelligence than between instrumental music reading ability and overall musical aptitude." Offer a logical basis for your reaction.

BIBLIOGRAPHY

1. Anastasiow, Nicholas, and Robert Shambaugh, "Experimental Use of Pre-Instrumental Music Melody Instruments," *Journal of Research In Music Education,* XIII (1965), 246–48.

2. Becker, William, "The Effects of Overlearning, Initial Learning Ability and Review upon the Music Memory of Junior High School Cornet and Trumpet Players." Unpublished Ph.D. dissertation, University of Iowa, 1962.

3. Brown, Roberta W., "A Comparison of the 'Whole,' 'Part,' and 'Combination' Methods of Learning Piano Music," *Journal of Experimental Psychology,* XI (1928), 235–47.

4. Burroughs, G. E. R., and J. N. Norris, "Factors Involved in Learning a Simple Musical Theme," *British Journal of Educational Psychology,* XXXII (1962), 18–28.

5. Colby, M. G., "Instrumental Reproduction of Melody by Pre-school Children," *Journal of Genetic Psychology,* XLVII (1935), 413–30.

6. Colwell, Richard, "An Investigation of Musical Achievement Among Vocal Students, Vocal-Instrumental Students, and Instrumental Students," *Journal of Research in Music Education,* XI (1963), 123–30.

7. Cramer, W. F., "The Relation of Maturation and Other Factors of Achievement in Beginning Instrumental Music Performance at the Fourth Through Eighth Grade Levels." Unpublished Ed.D. dissertation, The Florida State University, 1958.

8. Diamond, Robert M., and Claudette Sorel, *An Independent Learning Approach to Piano Sight Reading.* Washington, D.C.: Department of Health, Education, and Welfare. Office of Education, Bureau of Research. Ed. 023–299, 1968.

9. DiFronzo, Robert Francis, "A Comparison of Tachistoscopic and Conventional Methods in Teaching Grade Three Music Sight-Playing on a Melody Wind Instrument." Unpublished Ph.D. dissertation, University of Connecticut, 1966.

10. Engel, Alvin and Cynthia Engel, "The Effects of Musical Distraction upon the Performance Efficiency of Children," *Journal of Educational Research,* LVI (1962), 45–47.

11. Fred, Bernhart G., "The Instructional Value of an Exploratory String Instrument in a Fourth Grade." Unpublished Ph.D. dissertation, Northwestern University, 1956.

12. Froseth, James, "An Investigation of the Use of Musical Aptitude Profile Scores in the Instruction of Beginning Students in Instrumental Music." Unpublished Ph.D. dissertation, University of Iowa, 1968.

13. Gordon, Edwin, *Musical Aptitude Profile Manual.* Boston: Houghton Mifflin Company, 1965.

14. Gordon, Edwin, "Taking Into Account Musical Aptitude Differences Among Beginning Instrumental Music Students," *American Educational Research Journal,* VII (1970), 41–53.

15. Gursch, Kenneth Urial, "Evaluation in Instrumental Music Performance: An Individual Approach," *Council for Research in Music Education,* IV (1965), 21–29.

16. Hatfield, Warren, "An Investigation of the Diagnostic Validity of MAP with Respect to Instrumental Performance." Unpublished Ph.D. dissertation, University of Iowa, 1967.

17. Jacobs, Camille, "Investigation of Kinesthetics in Violin Playing," *Journal of Research in Music Education,* XVII (1969), 112–14.

18. Jacobsen, O. I., "An Analytic Study of Eye Movements in Reading Vocal and Instrumental Music," *Journal of Musicology,* III (1942), 223–26.

19. Johnson, Gordon B. "Negative Practice on Band Instruments: An Exploratory Study," *Journal of Research in Music Education,* X (1962), 100–104.

20. Juhacy, A., "Zur Analyse des musikalischen Wiedererkennens," *Zeitschrift fur Psychologie,* XCV (1924), 142–80.

21. Kersey, Robert E., "Effects of an Exploratory Program in Instrumental Music on the Aural Perception of Instrumental Timbre," *Journal of Research in Music Education*, XIV (1966), 303–8.

22. Kovacz, S., "Untersuchungen über das musikalische Gedachtnis," *Zeitschrift fur Angewandte Psychologie*, XI (1916), 113–35.

23. Lannert, Violet, and Marguerite Ullamn, "Factors in the Reading of Piano Music," *American Journal of Psychology*, LVIII (1945), 91–99.

24. Lowery, H., *The Background of Music*. London: Hutchinson & Co. (Publishers) Limited, 1952.

25. Luce, John R., "Sight-Reading and Ear-Playing Abilities as Related to Instrumental Music Students," *Journal of Research in Music Education*, XIII (1965), 101–9.

26. Lund, Victor E., *The Evaluation of Electronic Self-Instruction on the Piano Keyboard*. Washington, D.C.: Department of Health, Education, and Welfare. Office of Education, Bureau of Research. Ed. 016–391, 1966.

27. Mason, James A., "Comparison of Solo and Ensemble Performances with Reference to Pythagorean, Just, and Equi-Tempered Intonations," *Journal of Research in Music Education*, VIII (1960), 31–38.

28. Nelson, C. B., "An Experimental Evaluation of Two Methods of Teaching Music in the Fourth and Fifth Grades," *Journal of Experimental Education*, XXIII (1955), 231–38.

29. Nelson, C. B., "Follow-up of an Experimental Teaching Method in Music at the Fourth and Fifth Grade Levels," *Journal of Experimental Education*, XXIV (1956), 283–89.

30. Noble, Robert F., *A Study of the Effects of a Concept Teaching. Curriculum on Achievement in Performance in Elementary School Beginning Bands*. Washington, D.C.: Department of Health, Education and Welfare. Office of Education, Bureau of Research. Ed. 028–189, 1969.

31. O'Brien, C. C., "Part and Whole Methods in the Memorization of Music," *Journal of Educational Psychology*, XXXIV (1943), 552–60.

32. Rubin-Rabson, Grace, "Mental and Keyboard Overlearning in Memorizing Piano Music," *Journal of Musicology*, III (1941), 33–40.

33. Rubin-Rabson, Grace, "Studies in the Psychology of Memorizing Piano Music I: A Comparison of the Unilateral and the Coordinated Approaches," *Journal of Educational Psychology*, XXX (1939), 321–45.

34. Rubin-Rabson, Grace, "Studies in the Psychology of Memorizing Piano Music II: A Comparison of Massed and Distributed Practice," *Journal of Educational Psychology*, XXXI (1940), 270–84.

35. Rubin-Rabson, Grace, "Studies in the Psychology of Memorizing Piano

Music III: A Comparison of the Whole and the Part Approach," *Journal of Educational Psychology*, XXXI (1940), 260–376.

36. Rubin-Rabson, Grace, "Studies in the Psychology of Memorizing Piano Music IV: The Effects of Incentive," *Journal of Educational Psychology*, XXXII (1941), 45–54.

37. Rubin-Rabson, Grace, "Studies in the Psychology of Memorizing Piano Music V: A Comparison of Pre-Study Periods of Varied Length," *Journal of Educational Psychology*, XXXII (1941), 101–12.

38. Rubin-Rabson, Grace, "Studies in the Psychology of Memorizing Piano Music VI: A Comparison of Two Forms of Mental Rehearsal and Keyboard Learning," *Journal of Educational Psychology*, XXXII (1941), 593–602.

39. Rubin-Rabson, Grace, "Studies in the Psychology of Memorizing Piano Music VII: A Comparison of Three Degrees of Overlearning," *Journal of Educational Psychology*, XXXII (1941), 688–95.

40. Rubin-Rabson, Grace, "Studies in the Psychology of Memorizing Piano Music VIII: The Inhibitory Influence of the Same and of Different Degrees of Learning," *Journal of Musicology*, V (1947), 25.

41. Rubin-Rabson, Grace, "The Influence of Analytical Prestudy in Memorizing Piano Music, *Archives of Psychology*, XXXI (1937), 1–53.

42. Suzuki, Shinichi, *Nurtured by Love*. New York: Exposition Press, 1969.

43. Taylor, C. G., "Prevailing Practices in the Supervision of Instrumental Music," *Journal of Research in Music Education*, X (1962), 30–38.

44. Waa, Loren, "An Experimental Study of Class and Private Methods of Instruction in Instrumental Music." Unpublished D.Ed. dissertation, University of Illinois, 1965.

45. Wakeham, G., "Query on a Revision of the Fundamental Law of Habit Formation," *Science*, LXVIII (1928), 135–36.

46. Yarborough, William, "Demonstration and Research Program for Teaching Young String Players," *Council for Research in Music Education*, XII (1968), 26–31.

CHAPTER NINE

the evaluation of musical achievement

A comprehensive music achievement test may be used for various purposes. When it is to be used for 1) measuring students' normative and idiographic standing on different aspects of musical achievement, 2) determining if students' musical achievements are appropriate to their levels of musical aptitude, 3) evaluating students' musical development from year to year, and 4) comparing the musical achievement among individuals and groups of students, the content validity of the battery must first be examined and considered appropriate. That is, item content should receive major attention when evaluating the practicability of an achievement battery. Of course, the teacher should not overlook the possibility that the content of an achievement test, while he may not think it suitable, may, in fact, be suggestive of what he might more appropriately be teaching his students. In this sense, the structure of a comprehensive test could serve as a curricular *guide* before the battery is used for evaluative purposes.

If students' achievement in unique course content is to be evaluated, a teacher-made test should be used for this purpose. This is so because different groups of students are generally exposed to specific musical facts. As a result, a professionally developed comprehensive test, intended for general use, cannot be expected to cover adequately that specific curricular content stressed by an individual teacher. A particular problem prevails in regard to music theory because not all students are taught the same definitions for all musical signs and symbols. If a specially devised test is used, the responsibility of adequately developing the test and deriving norms, of course, remains with the teacher. Recommendations and standards for constructing both objective and essay tests and rating scales may be found in Ebel (5), Edwards and Scannell (6), and Lehman (13).

Comprehensive standardized music achievement tests, such as *EMAT* (4), are best for assessing students' aural perception and music literacy ability. If a teacher possesses such measures of students' perceptional and literacy achievement, she can then more properly develop a course of study in music, for example, from which a class and individual students may profit most.

As with aptitude batteries, raw scores for the various subtests of an achievement battery are properly converted to standard scores to facilitate interpretation of test results. A raw score simply reports how many items a student answered correctly on a test. Because raw score means and standard deviations cannot be expected to be the same for each subtest in a battery, students' raw scores on any two subtests do not have the same meaning. However, when all subtest raw scores are converted to the same normative scores—such as standard scores, percentile ranks, or grade equivalents—a student's performance on any one subtest can be quickly and meaningfully compared to his performance on any other subtest in the battery. And the significance of the difference between the subtest scores of different students can be more efficiently interpreted. Standard scores also make it possible to evaluate more appropriately an individual student's development in musical achievement from year to year, as well as that of an entire class.

Particularly for evaluating growth and relative standing in musical achievement, a multilevel test battery (preferably one which provides corresponding subtests that differ in complexity from level to level) is most functional. Through the use of such a battery, musical achievement can be evaluated with tests that are most appropriate in content to students' specific level of musical development.* A wide-range single-level test, which is repeatedly given to students from year to year for

---

* A multilevel musical achievement battery, the *Iowa Tests of Music Literacy,* has recently been published by the Bureau of Educational Research and Service, The University of Iowa, Iowa City, Iowa.

the purpose of evaluating their development in achievement, is an inefficient test. Such a test must, by definition, include a reasonable number of items which are too difficult for younger students to answer and some items which are too easy for older students. A multi-level battery is not wasteful of time as is a single-level test because in the former, students are asked to consider only those concepts which may be properly expected to challenge them. As a consequence, a given level of a multi-level battery includes a valid and more abundant assortment of items which relate to specific musical content associated with a particular aspect of an organized music program.

Furthermore, a multi-level battery comprised of various subtests also facilitates the identification of specific areas in which a class or individuals may especially need remedial work. Because we know that learning is a sequential developmental process, a multi-level battery becomes particularly valuable for developing course objectives in that scores reflect students' comprehension of formative capabilities, those which provide the foundation for more complex understanding. Whether professionally developed or teacher-made, a test should serve the necessary function of providing a unique type of learning situation for the examinees.

It should be pointed out that there are published tests available for measuring specialized aspects of musical achievement. For example, the *Watkins-Farnum Performance Scale* (24) is designed to assess individual progress in instrumental music performance, and the *Oregon Musical Discrimination Test,* recently revised by Long (15), measures the ability to discriminate between the work of an artist and that of a psychologist-musician who has made a deliberate attempt to mutilate a masterpiece. A description of these tests and other achievement tests and scales can be found in Lehman (13) and Whybrew (26).

THE GRADING PROCESS

In most elementary and secondary schools in the United States where grades are awarded in music, they are reported in the form of A, B, C, D, or F. Not only does this five-point system fail to provide for a precise interpretation but, more importantly, grades, in and of themselves, do not describe the criteria by which a student was evaluated. Specifically, it is difficult to determine if grade reports refer to a student's tonal achievement, his rhythmic achievement, his singing ability, his expressive techniques, his instrumental performance ability, or his attitude about music or toward the teacher. In some cases it may even be that students are graded only on musical potential or extracurricular activities such as keyboard technique.

Ideally, grades in music are based on students' comparative *musical achievement* which corresponds to one or more closely defined *behavioral objectives* of the school music program. As behavioral objectives change from semester to semester or from grade to grade, student progress should be reported in terms of the current goals. Only when the goals are understandable to the student and the parent (and of course to the teacher), can the positive functions of grades be served. Basically, grades should describe a student's relative achievement compared to that of other students in a class either on the basis of standards set by the class or by preconceived standards developed by the teacher.

The value of awarding grades lies in more than the information provided students and their parents. Grades should serve to motivate students in a positive way to achieve in accordance with their potential and should guide parents in developing realistic expectations for their children and in acquiring an interest in the school music program. Well-defined grades can stimulate and aid parents to offer remedial or supplementary instruction to their children within the home environment. Often this type of activity evolves from and stimulates worthwhile parent-teacher conferences. Through such occurrences the music program cannot help but gain respect.

It can also be expected that teachers will gain much from the grading process. Most important in this regard is that teachers need to clarify the behavioral objectives of their course in order to evaluate and report students' progress in the achievement of program goals. If achievement in certain aspects of a program is difficult to assess, it might be suggested that particular goals are in need of clarification or that they are completely unrealistic and therefore might be abandoned. It makes little sense to say that something can be taught which does not lend itself to evaluation.

An efficient way in which student music achievement can be recorded and reported is described in Illustration 1. Only three letters are used: E for excellent, S for satisfactory, and P for poor. (However, if it is mandatory, such as might be the case in a secondary school, that the traditional five-letter system be used, A, B, and C can be substituted for E, S, and P, respectively, and be given the former definitions.) With this type of form, appropriate objectives (in parentheses in Illustration 1) can be inserted which correspond to the sequence of the course of study in general music classes or performance groups. Students will receive an E, S, or P relating to each behavioral objective and also one of these letters for his composite (average) achievement at the end of each semester. An abundance of composite S's should be assigned, only a few E's, and occasionally a P. For the latter, such an occasion might be when a student receives a P for each aspect of achievement including attitude. However, there should be no restriction on the number of E's or P's given as they relate to specific behavioral objectives. As a result of evaluating specific aspects of musical achievement, the teacher becomes more familiar with students' musical accomplishments and is thereby better able to provide for their individual musical needs. When the teacher begins the evaluation process early in the semester, she becomes aware of those students with whom she is not well acquainted and can then make provision for immediate evaluation of their achievement. This, of course, facilitates a good teaching-learning situation.

To help parents better interpret the evaluation of the musical achievement of their children, the class composite achievement distribution may be reported in the space provided in Illustration 1. Parents should know, for example, how many students in a class received composite E's, S's, and P's, to understand the implication of these grades. If only three students in a class of thirty were awarded an E and their child was one of the three, parents certainly are more entitled to be proud of this level of achievement than if twenty students received an E.

If desired, students' musical aptitudes may be reported on the form. For students in grade four and above, national, regional, or local norm *percentile ranks* should be reported for those dimensions of aptitude which correspond to specific aspects of achievement (as defined by course objectives). In this way, realistic expectations for level of accomplishment become more obvious to the parent as well as to the teacher. Through a comparison of achievement and aptitude results, it is possible to determine whether or not a student's achievement corresponds to his potential.

SUMMARY

Comprehensive musical achievement test batteries may be used for 1) measuring students' normative and idiographic standing on different aspects of musical achievement, 2) determining if students' musical achievements are appropriate to their levels of musical aptitude, 3) evaluating students' musical development from year to year, and 4) comparing the musical achievement among individuals and groups of students. A multi-level test battery is best for meeting all of these purposes.

Grades in music should be based on students' comparative *musical achievement* which corresponds to one or more clearly defined behavioral objectives of the school music program. Grades also serve to motivate students and teachers, and to inform parents of the nature of their chil-

NAME _____ TEACHER _____ GRADE _____

E = Excellent
S = Satisfactory
P = Poor

MUSICAL ACHIEVEMENT

SEMESTER ONE		SEMESTER TWO	
(Tonal readiness)		(Tonal literacy)	
(Rhythm readiness)		(Rhythm literacy)	
(Singing ability)		(Musical expression)	
(Attitude)		(Attitude)	

COMPOSITE		COMPOSITE	

MUSICAL APTITUDE

TONAL	
RHYTHMIC	
EXPRESSIVE	

COMPOSITE	

CLASS COMPOSITE ACHIEVEMENT DISTRIBUTION

	SEMESTER ONE	SEMESTER TWO
E		
S		
P		

COMMENTS:

_____

_____

_____

_____

ILLUSTRATION 1

dren's growth. To be most useful, grades in musical achievement should be compared to each student's level of musical aptitude.

STUDY GUIDE

1. Differentiate between musical achievement and musical aptitude.
2. If you were to write a musical achievement test, describe, with specific test items, how you would comprise its content?
3. Differentiate among the terms "interpretation," "evaluation," and "grading."
4. Consider that your child received a grade of B in music. Interpret the meaning of that grade.
5. Explain why the development of course goals, behavioral objectives, lesson plans, evaluation and interpretive processes, and the awarding of grades are interrelated.

BIBLIOGRAPHY

1. Blommers, Paul, and E. F. Lindquist, *Elementary Statistical Methods in Psychology and Education.* Boston: Houghton Mifflin Company, 1960.

2. Buck, Percy, *Psychology for Musicians.* London: Oxford University Press, 1961.

3. Buros, Oscar, *The Sixth Mental Measurements Yearbook.* Highland Park, N.J.: The Gryphon Press, 1965.

4. Colwell, Richard, *Elementary Music Achievement Tests.* Chicago: Follett Publishing Company, 1967.

5. Ebel, Robert, *Measuring Educational Achievement.* Englewood Cliffs: Prentice-Hall, Inc., 1965.

6. Edwards, Jack, and Dale Scannell, *Educational Psychology; The Teaching-Learning Process.* Scranton, Pennsylvania: International Textbook Company, 1968.

7. Farnsworth, Charles, *Short Studies in Musical Psychology.* London: Oxford University Press, 1930.

8. Farnum, Stephen, *Farnum Music Notation Test.* New York: The Psychological Corp., 1953.

9. French, John et al., *Standards for Educational and Psychological Tests and Manuals.* Washington: American Psychological Association, Inc., 1966.

10. Gordon, Edwin, *Iowa Tests of Music Literacy*. Iowa City: The University of Iowa Bureau of Educational Research and Service, 1970.

11. Kwalwasser, Jacob, and G. M. Ruch, *Kwalwasser-Ruch Test of Musical Accomplishment*. Iowa City: University of Iowa, 1924.

12. Kwalwasser, Jacob, *Tests and Measurements in Music.* Boston: C. C. Birchard Co., 1927.

13. Lehman, Paul, *Tests and Measurements in Music*. Englewood Cliffs: Prentice-Hall, Inc., 1968.

14. Lindquist, E. F. et al., *Educational Measurement*. Washington: American Council on Education, 1951.

15. Long, Newell, "A Revision of the University of Oregon Music Discrimination Test." Unpublished Ed.D. dissertation, Indiana University, 1965.

16. Lyman, Howard, *Test Scores and What They Mean*. Englewood Cliffs: Prentice-Hall, Inc., 1963.

17. Madison, Thurber et al., *Perspectives in Music Education*. Washington, D.C.: Music Educators National Conference, 1966.

18. Mueller, Kate, "Studies in Music Appreciation," *Journal of Research in Music Education,* IV (1956), 3–25.

19. Pinkerton, Frank, "Talent Tests and Their Application to the Public School Instrumental Music Program," *Journal of Research in Music Education,* XI (1963), 75–80.

20. Swinchoski, Albert, "A Standardized Music Achievement Test Battery for the Intermediate Grades," *Journal of Research in Music Education,* XIII (1965), 159–68.

21. Swisher, Walter, *Psychology for the Music Teacher*. Boston: Oliver Ditson Company, 1927.

22. Teplov, B. M., *Psychologie des Aptitudes Musicales*. Paris: Presses Universitaires de France, 1966.

23. Thorndike, Robert, and Elizabeth Hagen, *Measurement and Evaluation in Psychology and Education*. New York: John Wiley & Sons, Inc., 1969.

24. Watkins, John, and Stephen Farnum, *The Watkins-Farnum Performance Scale*. New York: Hal Leonard Music, Inc., 1954.

25. Watkins, John, *Objective Measurement of Instrumental Performance*. Contributions to Education, Number 860. New York: Teachers College, Columbia University, 1942.

26. Whybrew, William, *Measurement and Evaluation in Music*. Dubuque, Iowa: William C. Brown Company, Publishers, 1962.

epilogue

To the extent that the reader has appropriately perceived the contents of this book, he should recognize that the afterthoughts in which he is now, and hopefully will continue to be, engaging would be properly defined by the author as evidence of conceptualization.